An Archer Looks
at the Bible

An Archer Looks
at the Bible

A study of the literal and
figurative allusions to the bow
and arrow

David Finnemore Hill

The Pentland Press
Edinburgh – Cambridge – Durham

First published in 1994 by
The Pentland Press Ltd
1 Hutton Close
South Church
Bishop Auckland
Durham

ISBN 1-85821-167-0

Front cover: The Arrow of Victory – followed by
the death of Elisha, early eighth century B.C. (p. 33).
Frank Dicksee (1853–1928) produced this in 1898
for The International Bible. In 1924 he became President of The Royal Academy and was knighted in the
following year. (Courtesy, The British Museum and
The Paul Mellon Centre for Studies in British Arts.)

Typeset by Carnegie Publishing, 18 Maynard St., Preston
Printed in Great Britain by Bookcraft (Bath) Limited

To

Janet

Vanessa and Francesca

Contents

List of Illustrations ix

Foreword xi

Introduction 1

Chapter I.   **Literal**

  Before the Monarchy 5

  Saul 15

  David 20

  The Bronze Bows 23

  The Kings 29

    Asa 29

    Jehoshapha 30

    Ahab 31

    Joram 34

    Jehu 35

    Jehoash 37

    Uzziah (Azariah) 39

    Hezekiah 42

    Josiah 44

  Nehemiah 46

  The Prophets 47

    Amos 48

    Hosea 48

    Isaiah 49

    Jeremiah 51

    Ezekiel 53

    Second Isaiah 56

Third Isaiah   57
Second Zechariah   57
The Apocrypha   58

Chapter II.   **The Bow and Arrow as a Figure of Speech**
Part I.   God Against Enemies   63
              God Against Friends   68
              Two Special Texts   71
Part II.   Proverbial   73
              The Wicked   78
              Miscellany   81
              Faith   84

Some Notes on the Hebrew   87

Epilogue   89

Archery References   94

Appendix I.   The Revolution   98

Appendix II.   The Apocrypha   100

Bibliography and Abbreviations   105

Acknowledgements   106

List of Illustrations

The Arrow of Victory   front cover
Bronze arrowheads   3
B-bow and shoulder quiver   4
Later bronze arrowhead   14
Iron arrowheads   19
Two solid bronze bows   26
Indian steel bows   28
Jehu shooting at Joram   37
Iron arrowheads from Lachish   42
Statue of Gog   55
Indian incendiary arrows   67
Vision of a White Horse   90
Iron arrowheads and a shaft from Masada   91

Maps

Tribal Allotments   11
Map of Palestine in Old Testament times
    (by coutesy of Oxford University Press)   107
Map of the Persian Empire
    (by coutesy of Oxford University Press)   108

Foreword

by Robert Hardy
C.B.E., M.A., Hon. D. Litt.

D R HILL's study is a revelation. Not only does it record and analyse the 130-odd general references to archery, both factual and figurative in the Old Testament, but it provides for those who know the Bible not at all, or those who know it in passing, or even who know it well, a fascinating historical commentary which puts events into a comprehensible order and throws a great deal of light into the labyrinthine shadows of the Old Testament stories.

The rarity of allusions to archery in the New Testament is perhaps explained by the closer focus of its historical frame, covering so little ground in comparison with the Old Testament, a span of time that is exclusively within the period of Roman supervision, when the use of archery was severely controlled and limited in large measure to the armed forces, as it was during much of the Middle Ages in Britain. In any case, the New Testament is concerned with the beginning of Christianity and not about battles and warfare.

We hear of David's special archer corps who could shoot with either hand, an achievement I have long suspected of our best practitioners during the apogee of the longbow; of bronze bows; or arrows woundings that recall the dead of Nebhep Re; of sharpshooters; of arrow-throwing siege engines; of 280,000 men 'that carried shields and drew bows' from the tribe of Benjamin, reminding us of the hopeless pursuit of likely numbers in all early history; of defending troops 'holding spears, shields and bows, that conjures a vivid picture of extraordinary confusion on the ramparts. "At the sound of the horsemen and archers the whole country is in flight" says Jeremiah, and he might be writing of France in the fourteenth century.

Ecclesiasticus warns of the dangers of a precocious daughter in a neat and evocative phrase: "She will open her arms to every embrace, and her quiver to the arrow." From jumping Jehoshaphat to the apocalyptic archer on a white horse, it is all here, pinned and exhibited for our delight and instruction. Every archer, every historian, every bibliophile should take pleasure in it, and most other readers as well.

Introduction

THIS little book traces its origin to a fairly long article I wrote for *Archery News* (Vol. 24:1; May 1945). Fortunately, I had previously noted down most of the references to the bow and arrow as I worked my way through the Bible, for I had no access to a concordance – at least, not to a comprehensive one.

Many readers will be aware of the numerous references to bows and arrows in the Psalms, but it may come as a surprise that there are about 120 archery allusions in the Old Testament. The quantity is only approximate because a number are repetitions and sometimes the Hebrew text is corrupt – the New Engligh Bible has relegated some to footnotes and deleted others altogether. In addition, there are eleven references in the Apocrypha, but understandably only three or four in the New Testament.

After the book was supposedly finished, but before publication, The Revised English Bible appeared. Hence all the allusions were able to be checked and alteration or comment made where necessary. Similarly, references were also checked in The New Jerusalem Bible, which came out nineteen years after the first edition. As might be expected, there are gains and losses from our viewpoint.

There are two principal categories. The literal one deals with armies and related topics such as assassination. The other main chapter contains figurative or proverbial texts, about half of them depicting God as an Archer. On the whole they are down to earth rather than the flowery archery metaphors of the Greek poet Pindar in the fifth century. References in the Apocrypha are included and there is an Epilogue for the New Testament.

The order in which the historical passages are looked at is chiefly that of the Bible itself – apart from I and II Chronicles. I have tried to arrange the prophets, however, in the order of their ministries.

To cut down the number of footnotes, simple Bible references have been inserted in the main text. In general, these notes relate to non-archery matters.

Dates and centuries are B.C., unless otherwise stated.

I would like to thank The Reverend D. Keith Innes, M.A., B.D., now Vicar of Doddington, Kent, for his contribution on the Hebrew aspect.

I am also indebted to The Reverend Philip H. Buss, M.A., former Vicar of Old Woking, for reading through the text and for making a number of valuable comments.

I am grateful to my former colleague, Mr Temple A. Smyth, B.A., previously of Dane Court, Pyrford, and St Andrew's School, Woking, for many improvements in my text after reading two drafts; also to Mr Frederick H. Lake, F.L.A., Honorary Librarian of The Simon Archery Foundation, and to Mr Edward McEwen, Editor of *The Journal of the Society of Archer-Antiquaries*; and to Mrs Elaine English for her accurate typing.

Finally, I must express my deep gratitude to Mrs A. Wendy Hodkinson, Honorary Keeper of The Simon Archery Collection, The Manchester Museum, not only for recommending a general change in strategy, but for countless particular suggestions, almost all of which were accepted.

D. J. F. H.
Woking,
England.

Bronze tanged arrowheads of approximately 2,000 B.C., a century or two before Ishmael, son of Abraham, the first archer in the Bible.

They come from tombs on the Golan Heights, an area east of the Sea of Galilee which is thirty-one miles from north to south by twelve miles eastwards from the River. In Bible times this was possibly in the territory of Manasseh-beyond-Jordan.

(Courtesy, Israel Department of Antiquities and Museums).

An archer with a double-convex or 'B-bow', with quiver slung over his shoulder, and holding an axe with duck-bill blade. A caravan of Semites on the way to Egypt is depicted on a tomb at Beni-hasan. At c.1900 B.C., it is nearer the period of Ishmael than the arrowheads in the previous illustration. (From Yigael Yadin's *The Art of Warfare in Biblical Lands* (London, 1963), p. 166. Courtesy, Weidenfeld and Nicolson Limited.)

Chapter I

Literal

Before the Monarchy

The first allusion to archery in the Bible is a charming but indirect one. After the Flood, God places His bow in the sky as a sign to mankind that never again shall Earth suffer a total deluge. Dare we infer from the seven-colour rainbow that the Hebrews were more familiar with a simple bow than with a composite weapon? Perhaps the speculation is worth it, but one shies away from trying to be too clever.

> My bow I set in the cloud, sign of the covenant between myself and earth. When I cloud the sky over the earth, the bow shall be seen in the cloud ... the bow shall be in the cloud ...
>
> (Genesis 9:13, 14, 16).

There is another reference to the bow-in-the-cloud in the sixth century at the end of Ezekiel's extraordinary Vision of God (1:28).

The first real mention of anything to do with archery occurs twice in the story of Ishmael. Abraham and Sarah had been childless for many years. In desperation to get an heir, Abraham had contracted a kind of morganatic marriage with Hagar, Sarah's Egyptian slave, who produced Ishmael. Subsequently Sarah bore Isaac in her old age – he was to become the second of the three patriarchs 'Abraham, Isaac and Jacob'. Trouble came at a feast to celebrate Isaac's weaning, when Sarah saw Ishmael playing with the baby (a more likely translation than 'mocking').

Angry at such 'equality', she made Abraham expel slave girl and child. He reluctantly agreed when he was told by God that Ishmael was also to be the founder of a nation. Hagar wandered some twenty-five miles to the desert of Beersheba, which is the traditional southernmost point of 'Israel'.

When the waterskin ran out, "she thrust the child under a bush, and went and sat down some way off, about two bowshots away, for she said, 'How can I watch the child die?' So she sat some way off, weeping bitterly." Mercifully God showed her a well. A few verses on, it is said that Ishmael grew up to be an archer, went south to the Wilderness of Paran on the Sinai Peninsula, and that his mother found him a wife from her own country, Egypt (Genesis 21:15–21).

An intriguing question is "How far is a bowshot?" Like the alteration of the inner white to blue on the target face in 1851, it was probably so well known that scarcely anyone troubled to mention it. It is a vaguer term even than our 'stone's throw'. Perhaps it can be assumed that it means a shot at 45° for maximum distance and not merely effective range. The writer attempted to marshal some of the evidence from antiquity in an article in *The Journal of the Society of Archer-Antiquaries* (Vol. 6, 1963, pp. 29–30). See also Wallace McLeod, "The Range of the Ancient Bow" (*Phoenix* 19, 1965). There are several clues, of indirect value, in references to being beyond or within bowshot and a deduction from the width of the River Centrites (Eastern Tigris), and a recommendation for group practice at 60 yards (54.86 metres) – in motion! There is a fascinating inscription of the third century from Olbia, on the north coast of the Black Sea, which reads: "I say that the famous Anaxagoras, son of Demagoras, shot 282 orguias." However, this distance of 564 yards (515.72 metres) is more than a Grand Master Flight Shot for a man today. According to the Grand National Archery Society's Rules of Shooting (1987 edition, p. 46), it is 550 yards – and 450 for a woman. More relevant is a shot by Mithridates the Great, King of Pontus in Asia Minor in the first century B.C. King Mithridates "released an arrow from the corner of the roof and believed it exceeded a stadion by a little." (Strabo 14.1.23) A 'stadion' is 202 yards (184.71 metres), so a guess of an English furlong of 220 for the royal shot probably would not be far out.

To return to Hagar, it appears that she compromised: sufficiently far away not to see the child die, yet near enough to drive off birds of prey and smaller wild animals. From this point of view, the writer prefers the old reading of a single bowshot in the New Jerusalem Bible and in earlier versions rather than the 'two' of the New English Bible. Indeed, the Revised English Bible, published in 1989, has gone back to a single bowshot. The Greek version has *hōsei toxou bolēn* – literally, 'as if a throw of a bow'.[1]

To go back to her son, there would seem to be a link between the bowmanship of Ishmael and that of the warriors of Kedar, on the Syro-Arabian frontier south-east of Damascus. They are believed to be his descendants and named after his second son – one of twelve, as in the case of Jacob (re-named 'Israel' by God). Isaiah in the eighth century, in a brief oracle on Arabia, predicts the downfall of Kedar within a year: "Few shall be the bows left to the warriors of Kedar." He invites the inhabitants of Dedan and Tema, some 350 miles to the south, to bring water and food to the fugitives, "for they flee from the sword, the sharp edge of the sword, from the bent bow, and from the press of battle." (21:13–17) They are to be defeated by their own weapon.

In addition, the descendants of Jetur, Ishmael's tenth son, are identified with the Ituraeans (neighbours of the Phoenicians).

---

[1] This version of the Old Testament, originating in the third century B.C., is known as the Septuagint or LXX. It was so named because of the tradition that seventy scholars (half-a-dozen members from each tribe) translated it from Hebrew to Greek.

According to A. H. M. Jones in *The Oxford Classical Dictionary* (p. 463), they contributed three cohorts (500 men each) and a cavalry squadron of archers (also about 500 men) to the Roman army. He says that these Arabs were gradually broken of their predatory habits, but that they remained a primitive people, living in villages.

Isaac, the second son of the three original patriarchs, and Rebekah were the parents of Esau (hairy) and Jacob (catch-heel/supplanter). Although they were twins, Esau was technically the firstborn. He lost his 'birthright', however, when he sold it to Jacob 'for a mess of potage' after he returned famished from hunting. This gave him the nickname Edom (red), from the colour of the lentils. When Isaac was old and blind, he wanted to make sure before his death of blessing Esau: "Now then, take your weapons, your quiver and your bow, and go out to the field, and hunt game for me, and prepare for me savoury food, such as I love, and bring it to me that I may eat; that I may bless you before I die." (Genesis 27:3–4) Alas for them, Rebekah overhears this. She dresses up her favourite Jacob in Esau's clothes and places the skins of the kids, which she had prepared for the meal, on Jacob's hands and neck. She forgets, however, to instruct Jacob to disguise his voice – and Isaac nearly sees through the deception. Rebekah sends Jacob from Beersheba to his uncle's to avoid fratricide by an outraged Esau. The trek to Haran, some 450 miles to the north, proves worthwhile – for there he meets Rachel. Jacob in years to come is deceived in turn by his sons when they sell the seventeen-year-old Joseph to travelling traders. Esau was believed to be the founder of the Edomites south of the Dead Sea – capital Bozrah – just as Jacob's twelve sons become the twelve tribes of Israel. (Only one daughter is named – Dinah.) A saddened Isaac predicts to an embittered Esau the subservience of his descendants: "By your sword you shall live, and you shall serve your brother; but when you break loose, you shall break his yoke from your neck." (verse 40)

It is a short step from hunting to war. 'Joseph' was the most powerful of all the tribes and was subdivided into three. Ephraim, in central Canaan, became so important that the entire northern kingdom was often called by its name in later centuries. Manasseh had territory immediately to the north and on the east side of the Jordan. Joshua, Moses' successor, was to assign extra living-space to Ephraim and Manasseh (17:14–18). This is foreshadowed in the words of the aged Jacob to Joseph when he blesses his grandsons: "I give you one ridge [*lit.* shoulder] of land more than your brothers: I took it from the Amorites [Canaanite highlanders] with my sword and my bow." (Genesis 48:22) The coupling of these weapons is significant. With the Greeks and the Romans it would rather have been 'sword and spear', the bow being an important but secondary arm. From this and other passages one is entitled to deduce that archery played an important part in Hebrew warfare.

The last text in Genesis is to be found in one of the oldest pieces of Hebrew poetry. An indication of antiquity is the fact that Levi is not mentioned as the tribe of 'priests and Levites'. It may date from the transition period of the Judges – that is, between the wanderings in the wilderness and the monarchy – and therefore be as early as 1100 B.C. The later fortunes of the various tribes and their characteristics are put into the mouth of the dying patriarch Jacob (Israel). This is also addressed to the Joseph tribes, Ephraim and Manasseh. Here the archers are probably border raiders:

"Joseph is a fruitful tree by a spring
with branches climbing over the wall.
The archers savagely attacked him,
they shot at him and pressed him hard,
but their bow was splintered by the Eternal."

(Genesis 49: 22–24)

The Moffatt Bible translates verse 24 "but his own bow remains steady" and the Revised Version has a similar rendering.

The Revised English Bible has: "but Joseph's bow remained unfailing and his arms were tireless by the power of the Strong One of Jacob." Centuries pass between Genesis and Exodus. The Hebrews are now a small nation in Egypt. On the pretext that a state within a state could pose a threat in time of war, Pharoah enslaves the Israelites. He may be Rameses II in the thirteenth century, but some scholars believe it is another monarch a couple of hundred years earlier. The people have to make bricks with straw provided, and then find their own straw, while maintaining the same quota. God duly comes to the rescue with the Ten Plagues – some consider there were only eight, two being 'doublets'. Pharoah himself suffers from the Death of the Firstborn, the final plague, when the crown prince dies in the night. Moses and his brother Aaron lead the people through the so-called Red Sea, in which Pharoah and his host perish. It is in fact 'The Sea of Reeds' which is part of Lake Menzaleh, many miles north of what is popularly known as The Red Sea. Traditionally for forty years they are nomads in the desert until they reach Canaan, the Promised Land.

About halfway in their wanderings – geographically speaking – they encamp at the foot of Mt. Sinai, which is also known as Mt. Horeb. It is believed to be some fifty miles north from the tip of the Sinai Peninsula. Here Moses received the Ten Commandments on two stone tablets (Exodus 20). Because God was then believed to live on this mountain, it was regarded as holy. There was a prohibition on man or animal approaching – at least until the ram's horn sounded. So strong was the tabu that no contact was allowed with the offender at execution. "No hand shall touch him/it, but he shall surely be stoned or shot through." (Exodus 19:13) The Greek version has 'or shot down by a missile'. The verb contains the 'tox' element (*toxon*, a bow), combined with *kata* (down), but the projectile is simply a generic word for a missile (*bolis*). A few texts quote it in the Epistle to the Hebrews (12:20) in the New Testament.

Balaam – famous for the dialogue with his ass – was a God-fearing, non-Hebrew prophet. He appears to have come from Pethor near Carchemish on the Euphrates, although a variant text suggests that he was an Ammonite, a nation bordering on Moab. He was hired by Balak, King of Moab, which was east of the Dead Sea, some 350 miles to the south of Pethor. Balaam was directed to put a curse on migrating Israel. Despite his fee and the promise of reward, and after much to-ing and fro-ing, he could do no other than bless Israel.

According to the early versions, he predicts that Israel shall 'pierce them [the other nations] through with his arrows.' This is in line with the Greek Old Testament, "he shall shoot-down the enemy with missiles" (*bolisin* ... *katatoxeusei*) (Numbers 24:8). However, the New English Bible renders 'and smash their limbs in pieces' and the R.E.B. has a similar wording. They are joined by Moffatt and the Jerusalem Bible in rejecting the archery element, evidently because the devouring and crunching of bones suit the lion and lioness in the context far better than arrows. However, the *New Jerusalem Bible*, published nineteen years later, has inserted 'piercing them with his arrows'. If the restoration is true, then one has an appropriate early prophecy of the Hebrew use of the bow. The whole story is a rare (unique?) instance of foreigners dominating the scene.

In the course of his final charge before his death, Joshua, who succeeded Moses, reminds the people that 'the hornet' – perhaps panic or rumour of a plague we do not know about[2] – drove out the two kings of the Amorites (Sihon and Og) on the east of the Jordan, rather than they with their sword and bow (Joshua 24:12). Again these two weapons are coupled.

The traditional 'noise of archers' in Judges 5:11 (both A.V. and R.V.) is no longer considered a tenable translation. This is a pity, because Deborah's Song of Victory over the north Canaanites (based on Hazor) – virtually the whole of chapter 5 – is believed to be the oldest piece of writing in the Bible, dating to the twelfth century. The word that was rendered 'archers' is found only in this passage. The Revised Standard Version (1952) and the New English Bible (1970), following rather the Greek Old Testament, translate 'musicians' and 'players' respectively. The New Jerusalem Bible translates 'to the sound of the shepherds', pointing out in a footnote that the literal meaning is 'those who divide' (water, fodder or flocks). There is a pathetic piece of dramatic irony towards the end of the poem. The mother of the enemy Commander-in-Chief pictures him sharing out the spoils to account for his delayed return, whereas the reader knows that Sisera has been killed by Jael in her tent. In one text of the Greek version of verse 28 the word employed for the lattice through which the General's mother peered is *toxikon* – shot-hole or loop-hole, corresponding to the 'arbalestrina' in European castle walls.

The story of Samson and Delilah is well known, if only from the film starring Victor Mature and Hedy Lamarr. He was the Hercules of the Bible who 'ruled' Israel for two decades under

---

[2] It probably does not signify Pharaoh, whose symbol was a bee, for the Egyptians had withdrawn before the Hebrew invasion.

the Philistines in the earlier part of the eleventh century, the last
'Judge' but one. Samson belonged to the tribe of Dan in central
Canaan which was shortly to migrate to the far north – hence
the expression 'Dan to Beersheba', similar to our Land's End to
John O'Groats. He was a Nazirite, a holy man, allowed neither
alcohol nor haircuts – see Numbers 6. The secret of his strength
lay, of course, in his hair. He had the misfortune to fall in love
with Delilah, one of the enemy Philistines. Doubtless she was
flattered by the attentions of such a macho who was also leader
of his people. But she never seems to have returned his love, for
she was soon bribed to betray him. Assuming that the 'lords' of
all five cities of Philistia were involved, the payment was 5,500
silver pieces. Dr James Moffatt in his Old Testament translation,
possibly following Dummelow, reckoned this at £750. Updating
this 1935 sum by a factor of 35 (according to a financial journal-
ist), one gets £26,250 in contemporary value – a fortune to a
village maiden.

Three times Samson allows himself to be bound in what he
probably thinks is a lovers' game before he gives away his secret
after daily nagging.[3] He is captured, blinded, and put to forced
labour at Gaza. One of the rare appearances of 'bowstring'
occurs in the first of Samson's three jests: "If they bind me with
seven fresh bowstrings not yet dry, then I shall become weak
as any other man." (Judges 16:7) Seven is a sacred number,
associated with oaths. Almost certainly the strings in this part
of the world at this time would have been made of rawhide or
animal sinew. They would be dampened in the manufacturing
process. If a cord in this condition were to be used to tie
someone up, it would contract as it dried and make escape far

---

[3] In passing, it is interesting to note that, contrary to the impression given by
artists, it was apparently not Delilah who shaved off Samson's hair, but a man.
Note Dick Van Dyke's substantial wager in the 1967 film, *Fitzwilly*.

Late Bronze Age arrowhead found at Gaza, one of the five Philistine towns. It could be a Hebrew one; not necessarily shot by the enemy. 1550–1150 B.C. (Courtesy, The Manchester Museum).

more difficult.[4] Alternatively, flax or hair could have been employed for bowstrings, but the contraction property would not apply to these materials.

Samson? His hair grows again whilst in prison. When 'making sport' for his captors in the Temple of Dagon, he prays for strength, with grim humour, that he might be avenged for one of his two eyes. He heaves at the two central pillars – remains found at Gaza suggest wooden ones on stone bases – and demolishes the building. On the roof alone 3,000 had been watching, so he kills in death more than in his life. His younger brothers collect his corpse and bury it in the family tomb, some fifteen miles west of the later Jerusalem.

---

[4] I am grateful to the late Lt.-Cdr. W. F. Paterson, R.N., for drawing my attention to the question and to Mr Edward McEwen, Editor of *The Journal of The Society of Archer-Antiquaries*, for supplying an answer.

Saul

1032(?)–1010(?) B.C.

The Book of Judges deals with the transition period, lasting perhaps a century and a half, which is after the nomadic time in the desert and before the monarchy. Reflecting the ambivalence about kingship, the Bible records two separate traditions as to how it all began. In the better known one the prophet Samuel, under God, takes the initiative. He secretly anoints Saul, presumably in the former's home town of Ramah, when he had gone to find his father's asses. Possibly a month later he defeats the Ammonites on the other side of the Jordan and is duly crowned at Gilgal. In the other narrative the people clamour for a king, to be like other nations. Samuel, who is here portrayed as a judge rather than a prophet, takes a dim view of this demand. He regards it as a vote of no confidence in God and he paints a picture of oriental despotism which they can expect. This may be based on Canaanite practice, discovered in texts during the last two decades.

Perhaps, also, Samuel has in mind the three-year local 'reign' of the wicked Abimelech, as described in Judges 9. Nevertheless he reluctantly agrees and the king is chosen at Mizpah by lot: the tribe of Benjamin; the clan of Matri; Saul.

Why the question marks for Saul's reign? Unlike details in the Books of Kings, there are two problems in the opening verse of I Samuel 13. The Hebrew here is corrupt, for literally it says that Saul was a year old when he started to rule and that he did so for two years. The New English Bible has amended the text to read twenty-two years for the length of his reign.[5]

---

[5] One is less happy with the N.E.B. suggestion of fifty for his age at accession,

There are seven references to archers in the Books of Chronicles – a late work [6] dating to 300 B.C. or even after – which are not mere repeats of those in Samuel or Kings. Israel in the north is virtually ignored and the author writes a kind of commentary on the history of Judah and Benjamin in the south from a religious viewpoint.

Two interesting tribal allusions to archers are found in the genealogical introduction, which covers no fewer than nine chapters. It is stated that Reuben, Gad and the half tribe[7] of Manasseh (which had all settled on the east of Jordan) boasted swordsmen and bowmen to the tune of 44,760 (I Chronicles 5:18). The second one refers to Benjamin, which claimed: "The sons of Ulam were able men, archers, and had many sons and grandsons, a hundred and fifty."[8] (I Chronicles 8:40) In theory I Chronicles 1–9 run from Adam to Saul, but it would not be wise to relate the former statistic to the first King of Israel in the eleventh century. The number is far too large for just one region (Trans-Jordan) of a small country. If King Saul had had such forces at his disposal, and far more besides, one ventures to suggest that he would not have needed David's help in trying to rid Canaan of Philistine occupation. On the other hand, the modest 150

---

in view of the 'young' in I Samuel 9:2 and his exploits. The revised Septuagint text of thirty years seems more likely.

[6] Half-a-dozen generations (a dozen in some texts) are given after Zerubbabel, the Governor in 520, after the Exile; a contemporary of Alexander the Great, who died in 323, is mentioned; and the Hebrew is late. The name Chronicles was given by Jerome – in Hebrew 'Things of the days' and in Greek 'Things left out'.

[7] The two sections of Manasseh, on either side of the River, may have been caused by a population explosion. See the writer's Note in *The Expository Times*, February 1993 (104:5, pp. 140–1).

[8] Being the youngest of forty first-cousins, whose daughters are the youngest of seventy second-cousins, the writer can readily accept such a figure!

archers can be accepted for number and period, especially as they came from Saul's own tribe of Benjamin, which was a small one.

The friendship of David and Jonathan, Saul's son, has become proverbial, similar to that of Damon and Phyntias (not 'Pythias') in the Greek world. "So Jonathan and David made a solemn compact because each loved the other as dearly as himself. And Jonathan stripped off the cloak he was wearing and his tunic, and gave them to David, together with his sword, his bow and his belt." (I Samuel 18:3–4) How wonderful if this weapon were to turn up preserved in a grave, so one could learn its specifications!

In I Samuel 20 is the longest passage about archery in the entire Bible. David was in commmand of 1,000 warriors in Saul's army – approximately a lieutenant-colonel today, but perhaps more like a brigadier in status, having regard to the size of population then. He had married Princess Michal of Gibeah, so as well as a close friend he was now Jonathan's brother-in-law. David had been only too successful against the Philistines. Dancing women with tambourines had greeted him singing: "Saul has slain his thousands and David his ten thousands." This understandably incurred the jealous anger of the King and twice he tried to spear David while David was hoping to calm him down with the harp. Eventually David absents himself from a celebration at court, on the pretext of an annual family sacrifice at Bethlehem, to test Saul's intentions. Jonathan promises to let David, who is to hide in the fields, know the King's reaction: "Tomorrow is the new moon, and you will be missed when your place is empty. So go down at nightfall the day after tomorrow to the place where you hid on the evening of the feast and stay by the mound there. Then I will shoot three arrows towards it, as though I were aiming at a target. Then I will send my boy to find the arrows. If I say to him, 'Look, the arrows are on this side of you, pick them up', then you can come out of hiding. You will be quite safe, I swear it; for there will be nothing amiss. But if I say to the lad, 'Look, the arrows are on the other side of you, farther on', then the Lord has said that you must go; the Lord stand witness between us for ever to the pledges we have exchanged." It hardly needs saying that Jonathan would have gotten himself another weapon after he had presented David with his normal one. We do not have to suppose that the writer did not know about the gift or, like 'Homer nodding', had forgotten it!

Saul overlooks the absence at first, but on the second day he is furious when Jonathan explains where David is meant to be. After a heated argument about the friendship and the dynasty, when the King threatens to kill Jonathan himself, the crown prince leaves the table in a rage. "Next morning, Jonathan went out into the fields to meet David at the appointed time, taking a young boy with him. He said to the boy, 'Run and find the arrows; I am going to shoot.' The boy ran on, and he shot the arrows over his head. When the boy reached the place where Jonathan's arrows had fallen, Jonathan called out after him, 'Look, the arrows are beyond you. Hurry! No time to lose! Make haste!' The boy gathered up the arrows and brought them to his master; but only Jonathan and David knew what this meant; the boy knew nothing. Jonathan handed his weapons to the boy and told him to take them back to the town."[9] (I Samuel 20:18–23 and 35–40)

Near the end of the eleventh century (at the conclusion of I Samuel) a disastrous battle is fought against the Philistines at Mt. Gilboa. The mountain is some 1,600 feet high, twenty miles roughly south of Galilee. Not only did it virtually mark the end

---

[9] Why did Jonathan bother with the secret arrow message if he and David were to meet a few minutes later? It appears that another writer has inserted verses 40–2 down to 'for ever' (R.S.V.). If one reads the last sentence of chapter 20 immediately after verse 39, it makes perfect sense. Observe the Gore and Lowther Clarke commentaries and notice the Moffatt translation where double square brackets are used, denoting alleged interpolations. (See Bibliography.)

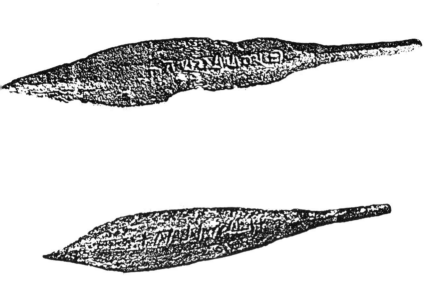

These might be thought to be javelin-heads if it were not for the inscription 'Hez Abd Lebaoth'. 'Hez' is 'arrow', while the name has been found among lists of archers discovered in Ugarit, north of Israel. Maybe the arrowheads were employed at the practice range or in competition to identify the bowman for scoring – much as we have names or initials and 'cresting' on the shaft.

The early Hebrew script can be dated to the twelfth or eleventh centuries B.C. As they were found at El-Khadr in the fifteen miles between Bethlehem and Hebron, the heads could have been used in the time and area of David and Jonathan. (Illustration from Yigael Yadin's *The Art of Warfare in Biblical Lands* (London, 1963), p. 353. Courtesy, the Estate of Yigael Yadin.)

of Saul's house, but it led to the evacuation of many towns in the region. Saul's army is routed; Jonathan and two other sons are killed. He was the first of several monarchs to be mortally wounded by the arrow. "The battle went hard for Saul, for some archers came upon him and he was wounded in the belly by the archers." (31:3) When his armour-bearer refuses to give the *coup de grâce*, Saul falls on his own sword. The Philistines nail his body to the wall of Beth-shan – the future Scythopolis, where retired Scythian archers were to be settled by Ptolemy II in the third century – but men from Jabesh-gilead cross the Jordan and go ten miles by night to recover the four royal corpses. This was an act of gratitude, for Saul had rescued them from the Ammonites which led to his kingship. The bodies were anointed and buried at Jabesh, but were later transferred across the river to the family grave at Zela, in Benjaminite territory.

David

1010(?)–c.970 b.c.

As Saul's dates are uncertain, it follows that the year of David's accession is also conjectural. One might be suspicious of the conventional 'forty' for the length of his reign – as well as for Saul (so Acts 13:21) and Solomon – were it not that the Bible specifies that David was King (at thirty) over Judah in Hebron for seven and a half years and over the united kingdom in Jerusalem for a further thirty-three years (II Samuel 5:1–5). It is a useful landmark for getting the history into some kind of perspective to remember that David was ruling in 1000 b.c.

Towards the end of David's status as a 'refugee' from Saul, Achish of Gath gave him Ziklag as a base. Presumably it was only his by Philistine conquest, because it belonged to Judah/Simeon and indeed was ten miles north of Beersheba, the traditional southern frontier. The account tells us not only the number of his archers and slingers, but also their names. One of the archer-slingers, Ismaiah of Gibeon, was a senior member of the Thirty, David's special warriors. Twenty-three, apparently under the command of two brothers, Ahiezer and Joash, "carried bows and could sling stones or shoot arrows with the left hand or the right." (I Chronicles 12:1–7) Once more they are Benjaminites and of course their number is acceptable.

It is of interest that in the last reference, in II Chronicles 14:8, 7:17, and in Psalm 78:9, the phrase used for archers is 'kissers of the bow'.[10] It suggests that the bowstring may have been brought to the lips of the archer as it is done today, rather than beyond them. Indeed, some archers have a 'kisser' on the string in order to line up with nose and chin to ensure that the drawing hand is in the same place each time. Of course, it may refer to a Hebrew custom of kissing the bow after a successful shot!

Saul's surviving son Ishbosheth has a two-year reign over part of Israel, but based east of Jordan, while David becomes King of Judah – but maybe only as vassal of the Philistines. He brings Jonathan's weapon into his famous Lament, which he orders to be taught to the people of his little realm and which was written down in the Book of Jashar ('Upright'), alas not extant. One verse runs:

> From the blood of the slain,
> from the fat of the mighty,
> The bow of Jonathan turned not back,
> And the sword of Saul returned not empty.
>
> (II Samuel 1:22)

It is disappointing, especially in view of the English ballad, that 'The Song of the Bow' found in the Revised Version cannot be

---

[10] I am grateful to The Revd Dr David Pennant, formerly of St John's Parish, Woking, for pointing this out to me and for clarifying several other references.

retained in verse 18. The Hebrew text here is hopelessly corrupt. 'Song' was added by the Revisers of 1885, replacing 'Use' in the Authorized Version of 1611. 'Bow', as a title, is clearly unsuitable to what follows and was omitted in the Greek Old Testament. At least two emendations have been suggested, but with no archery connections. The original Jerusalem Bible of 1966 omitted 'bow', as did Moffatt and N.E.B. Curiously enough, the New International Version and The New Jerusalem Bible have restored it: "(it is for teaching archery to the children of Judah ...)". The reader is referred to a footnote where it is rather dubiously implied that the psalm in II Samuel 22 accompanied archery exercises. Would it were certain!

Oddly enough, the New English Bible appears to be the only version which has an archery text at II Samuel 8:7. Translating 'shelet' as quiver rather than shield, it runs: "David took the gold quivers borne by Hadadezer's servants and brought them to Jerusalem." Hadadezer was King of Zobah, a region north of Damascus. The R.E.B. reverts to gold shields.

After the assassination of King Ishbosheth by two of his officers – wrongly thinking that David would be pleased – David is invited by the northern tribes to rule over them also. He is anointed at Hebron and duly moves his capital to Jerusalem, having captured it from the Jebusites.

The principal sin in David's life was a double one: adultery and, in effect, murder. Bathsheba had married Uriah, a Hittite and a member of the Thirty. Unlike the string of names of Canaanite peoples that often occurs, the Hittites had once been an empire – only realized a century ago by two scholars independently. It ceased around 1200 B.C. after over 500 years, to be followed by about thirty city-states. David from the palace rooftop saw Bathsheba washing herself and admired her body, so he had her brought to him ... When the King learns from her that she is pregnant, he sends for Uriah who is besieging Rabbah, the Ammonite capital over the Jordan, forty-five miles from Jerusalem. Twice he tries to get

Uriah to sleep with his wife. Uriah refuses, as he is on active
service, and thereby seals his own fate.

David orders Joab, his Commander-in-Chief, to station Uriah
in a vulnerable position and then desert him in the attack on
Rabbah (twenty-five miles east of the river), in order to marry
his widow. Dispatches are prepared, whose meaning is hidden
from the messenger. Joab anticipates David saying: "You must
have known there would be shooting from the wall." As Joab
expected, David pretended to be angry that his men went so near
the wall, to which the messenger responds: "The enemy massed
against us and sallied out into the open; we pressed them back
as far as the gateway. There the archers shot down at us from the
wall and some of your majesty's men fell; and your servant Uriah
the Hittite is dead."[11] (II Samuel 11:20; 23–4)

The Bronze Bows

Because of the probable connection with David in one of them,
it is convenient now to look at two references to metal bows
which have a possible relevance to warfare. The question is of
particular interest to those of us who shot in steel bows in the
nineteen-forties and fifties.[12] Strictly speaking, however, they are

---

[11] There follows the rebuke of the prophet Nathan (in the form of the parable
of the rich man and the poor man) and the death of the baby – with more than
a hint of an after-life at II Samuel 12:23. No wonder it has been speculated that
the great penitential Psalm 51 was composed by David on this occasion. The
sordid story is a prime example of God bringing good out of evil: Bathsheba,
in effect the Queen, becomes the mother of the future King Solomon.

[12] The writer used a 4-foot (121.9 cm) Swedish Seefab Scout bow, approximately 20 lb. draw-weight with a 25-inch (63.5 cm) arrow, which gave a point-
of-aim on the target at 70 yards (63.7 metres), before graduating to an adult
bow. Accles and Pollock requested an examination of it in case of help in their
production of Apollo bows. He used to shoot in the garden during the early

out of place here since both are figurative. The poet in II Samuel 22 (probably the earlier version of Psalm 18) simply meant that with Divine help he was able to do great things, while the author of Job 20 was just symbolically describing the fate of the sinner.

David – for it appears highly probable that he is the author – writes: "He trains my hands for war, so that my arms can bend a bow of bronze." (II Samuel 22:35) The LXX has variants, oddly enough for both references. For Psalm 18:34 it has: "and you made [*lit.* placed] my arms a bronze bow", while for II Samuel (which it calls 'II Kings') 22:35 it reads: "and has broken a bronze bow by my arm." The first reference (that is, the Hebrew one) could be taken literally and it may be that those who translated into Greek in the third century wished to make at least the Psalm allusion more obviously a metaphor.

Zophar, one of Job's so-called comforters, describes in a whole chapter of rhetoric what he considers is the doom of the wicked. In a string of calamities, "He shall fly from the iron weapon, and a bronze bow shall wound him. The arrow comes out at his back, the gleaming tip from his gall-bladder." (Job 20:24–5) The Hebrew and Greek texts vary – and so do the translators. The rendering here is eclectic, made up from three or four versions. It seems that the translators of the New English Bible consulted the metallurgists rather than the archaeologists, for they have dispensed with bows in both passages and have paraphrased respectively: "who trains my hands for battle, and my arms aim an arrow tipped with bronze" and 'pierced by a bronze-tipped arrow'.

The R.E.B. has redressed matters to some extent in the II Samuel passage by 'removing' the metal from the arrow and transferring it back to the bow where it belongs: "so that my arms can

---

1940s with David Wynne, the future sculptor, who also had a Scout bow which is now in the writer's possession. Wynne was made an O.B.E. in the New Year's Honours List last January.

aim a bronze-tipped bow". One might object in both versions that the purpose of the affirmation is that with God's assistance the writer is enabled to pull a strong bow – not merely to aim it. In view of the welcome change in II Samuel, it is a pity that the revisers have not altered the translation in Job as well. One can only guess that the reason is because the penetration of the arrow is alluded to in the next verse.

It should be noted in passing that bronzes came on the scene in the Euphrates/Tigris area between 3000 and 2500 B.C. and tin bronze was found in the Royal Graves at Ur dating to c. 2500 B.C. A tomb in Persia (Iran), whose date is put at 1300–1000 B.C., contained 3,000 bronze arrowheads of fifty different types.

To return to the two metal bows in metaphors. The Book of Job, concerned with the 'Problem of Pain' centuries before C. S. Lewis produced his book with this title, was probably written about 400 B.C. or somewhat later. (The *character* Job would appear to be older, as he is mentioned in the sixth-century Book of Ezekiel.) The Psalm, however, may be as early as 1000 B.C. – for if any were written by King David, no. 18 assuredly was one of them. If the eleventh century appears to be too early for such a figure of speech, there may be examples of the real thing – at least as part of the weapon – some 500 years before. There are possible allusions to such on tablets found at Nuzu (or Nuzi), in central Mesopotamia, 100 miles south-east of Nineveh. Yet caution must be exercised, because the word for bow (qastu or qaltu) is incompletely preserved and the reading is therefore uncertain. Further, it seems that only the 'side' was of bronze, so it may merely have been a decorative metal plate. These tablets are dated to the fifteenth or fourteenth centuries.

More likely to have inspired a metaphor in the Middle East were two 24-inch (60 cm) bows of solid bronze, one rectangular and the other irregularly elliptical in section. They were found during the 1897–9 excavations by Jacques de Morgan, G. Jéquier and G. Lampre at Susa (later capital of the Persian Empire), some

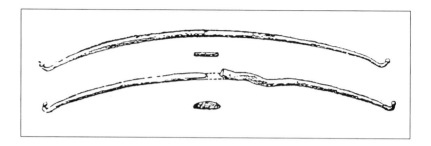

Two solid bronze bows (2/15 *grandeur naturelle*).

200 miles due east of Babylon. They were discovered in de Morgan's Trench no. 7 on the Citadel or Acropolis Tell. Apparently they date to long before the sack of Susa by the Assyrian Sennacherib in 696 B.C. Clearly these specimens would be far too small for use and were probably votive offerings – or possibly for ceremony. It is not known where they are today or even if they exist.[13]

The intriguing question is whether real bows were made of bronze. Dr Peter Pratt, Professor of Crystal Physics at Imperial College, University of London, conjectures:

> Are springs made of bronze today? Yes, phosphor-bronze is hard and strong with a high elastic modulus. As with spring steel, alloying, cold-working and heat treatment must be correct to prevent both ductile flow by bending and brittle fracture by microcracking or cleavage. Then the design of the bow would have to limit the tensile strain in

---

[13] Peter Pratt has recently drawn my attention to the bronze cross-bow on the 'burial chariot' of the Chinese Emperor Qin Shihuang, whose dynasty lasted from 246 to 210 B.C.. Professor Pratt reckoned that the span of the weapon was between 20 and 24 inches – not dissimilar to the length of the two Susa bows, many centuries earlier.

the back and the buckling strain in the belly, matching this to the draw-length of the archer. Could all this have been done in the Bronze Age? Yes possibly, but I imagine with many failures. The dimensions of the Susa bows are reminiscent of a crossbow[14] rather than a handbow and it seems unlikely that they influenced later designs, in particular that of the composite bow, in any obvious way.

As far as metal bows are concerned, centuries pass until India produced steel bows in the Mughal Period, which began in A.D. 1526. Two decades later Roger Ascham, tutor to the future Queen Elizabeth I, mentions in 1545 that the Turks had iron (!) and steel bows. In 1547 an inventory of Henry VIII lists a quantity of 'Turquy bowes of stele'. In 1588 a request was made to Council to re-introduce the bow, crossbow, and steel bow against the Spanish Armada – claiming a range of 400 yards for the latter weapon.

To return to metal bow design: in a subsequent letter, Professor Pratt suggests that the latest date for the Susa bronze bows at c.700 B.C. until A.D. 1526, when steel bows are first found, is too long a time-span for one to have influenced the other.

The late Lieutenant-Commander W. F. Paterson, R.N., when President of the Society of Archer-Antiquaries, drew my attention to later Indian steel bows. They are approximately a century and a half earlier than the cold-drawn, tapered, steel tube developed for archery in the 1930s in Sweden. An example of an Indian one in his collection was about two inches wide at mid-limb, but less than one tenth of an inch thick, and measuring only three feet (just under one metre) when strung. Although he admitted that

---

14 According to Douglas Elmy, *The Journal of the Society of Archer-Antiquaries*, Vol. 10 (1967), p. 41, the crossbow is found among the Chou invaders of China, c.1050 B.C. – the period of Samuel in the Bible. Hence, a Susa crossbow is possible, even if not very likely.

there were three variations in the basic design of these weapons, he saw no problem in doing much the same thing with a spring quality bronze. With regard to Professor Pratt's remarks, Cdr. Paterson said that tensile and buckling strains could be reduced by making the limb thin and getting the needed power by increasing the width. He suggested, regarding Professor Pratt's observation on design influence, that the earlier bronze bow may have influenced the later steel one, though there is no positive evidence to support this view.

All the above confirms the opinion of the present writer that the scholars translating

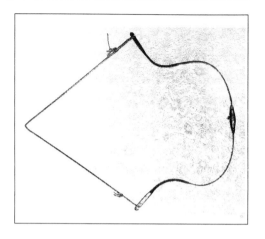

(Courtesy, Edward McEwen)

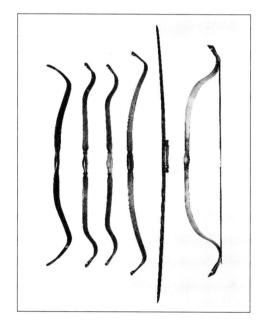

Indian steel bows.
(Courtesy, The Manchester Museum)

the New English Bible should have stuck to the text and not

substituted arrowhead for bow. It may well be that the 'bronze-tipped' arrow notion originated from an article by Sir Godfrey Driver in a German publication in 1950.

The revisers, as we saw, have improved one of the two texts. It is to be hoped that, in any future revision, 'bronze bow' will be re-instated and that, in the II Samuel and Psalm poems, 'draw' or 'pull', or even 'bend', will be substituted for 'aim'.[15]

*   *   *

To sum up. The evidence for Hebrew archery in the reigns of Saul and David is scanty enough. Signs of it in the time of Solomon in the tenth century, as far as the Bible is concerned, are non-existent.

The more-or-less united kingdom of Saul, David and Solomon split up on the latter's death in about 930 B.C. The division into the two monarchies of Judah and Israel is so important that an appendix has been added to explain the cause.

The Kings

And now to incidents or information in nine other reigns – five Judah and four Israel. The details about these monarchs are often

---

[15] I am most grateful to Dr J. E. Curtis, of the Department of Western Asiatic Antiquities at The British Museum, for a letter on the Nuzi tablets; to Mr Charles R. Blick of The Historical Metallurgy Society, for information on early bronze; to Professor Peter Pratt, of Imperial College, for a long letter on the whole question, further correspondence and for attempting to locate the Susa bows in France; and to the late Cdr. Paterson, for information contained in several letters. For more information on the subject, see Gad Rausing, The Bow – Some Notes On Its Origin and Development (Acta Archaeologica Lundensia, No. 6, 1967, pp. 90–1). The remarks on p. 137 under the heading 'The Copper Bow', however, are misleading in the view of the present writer.

very scrappy, since the writers are compiling a religious history. Frequently the Bible refers us to the Books of the Chronicles of the Kings of Judah (or of Israel), which unhappily no longer exist. The kings are placed in chronological order, with an obvious and minor exception where a son follows his father. The dates are at times conjectural. Mostly they follow the views of E. R. Thiele, which Professor John Gray adopted in Peake's Commentary on the Bible.

Asa

910–870 B.C. (Judah)

This monarch is looked upon favourably in general and especially because he instituted a religious reformation (the first of at least three), inspired by the prophet Azariah, son of Oded, in about 895. He expelled male cult prostitutes from shrines and removed all idols, burning his grandmother's obscene image and even demoting her from royal status. On the positive side, the Chronicler states that he ordered the worship of the Lord on pain of death. He also mentions that a great number from two or three northern tribes deserted to Asa when they learned that God was with him.

His story in II Chronicles 14–16 is a good example of expansion by the later writer. In I Kings 15 only sixteen verses are devoted to Asa, compared to forty-eight in the three chapters in Chronicles. In the latter there is an example of probably exaggerated figures in the 300,000 spearmen of Judah and "out of Benjamin, that carried shields and drew bows, 280,000" (lit. 'kissers of the bow') (II Chronicles 14:8) Similarly, it is difficult to credit the Ethiopian army which had penetrated as far as Mareshah, but twenty-five miles south-west of Jerusalem, with a million soldiers. This Cushite invasion or raid is not found in

'Kings'. However, the reference is supporting evidence for the bow in so-called 'little Benjamin'. This description, by the way, comes from Psalm 68:27. If 'their ruler' refers to King Saul who came from this tribe (as did the apostle Saul), then the poem, or part of it, is presumably eleventh-century.

Jehoshaphat

870–848 B.C. (Judah)

Again, Kings has only ten verses about Asa's son, another good monarch, as opposed to sixty-seven in Chronicles – leaving aside the chapter in both books on the alliance of Jehoshaphat and Ahab of Israel. According to the Chronicler, the tribe of Benjamin provided 200,000 armed with bows and shields, under their commander Eliada (II Chronicles 17:17). Once more, such figures must be treated with similar caution.

The reason for this is that Judah-and-Israel is a very small country, only about 145 miles 'from Dan to Beersheba' which became proverbial, as was mentioned earlier. Moreover, the census in Numbers 1 (which is why the book is so called) only gives 603,550 at verse 46 for the warrior males over twenty (not counting the Levites) – 159,000 fewer than Glasgow, Scotland! Even this is regarded as over-large, because it would imply a total population of some two million. Back in Egypt, only two midwives were mentioned for the entire nation – Exodus 1:15.

Ahab

874–853 B.C. (Israel)

Of all the Kings of Israel, Ahab probably comes in for the

greatest amount of stick. The historian, or perhaps an editor, puts it in a nutshell: "As if it were not enough for him to follow the sinful ways of Jeroboam son of Nebat (i.e., in setting up the two golden calves), he contracted a marriage with Jezebel daughter of Ethbaal, King of Sidon, and went and worshipped Baal." (I Kings 16:31) His infamous wife gave a new word to the English language – a shameless or profligate woman or, perhaps less frequently, a woman who puts garish colour on her face. Ahab appears more weak and peevish than wicked in the story of procuring Naboth's vineyard, since it is the Queen who has him framed on a charge of blasphemy and slander. Jezebel is a sort of Lady Macbeth – the power behind the throne. Indeed, the Bible itself says as much at I Kings 21:25. The one person who stood up to king and consort was Elijah the prophet. He was an heroic but a rather lonely and austere figure reminding one of John the Baptist, who seems to have modelled himself on the ninth-century seer (see Luke 1:17 and Matthew 17:12–13).

Syria had not handed back Ramoth-gilead, which was east of Jordan in the territory of Gad, in fulfilment of a treaty. When in 853 Jehoshaphat of Judah visited Ahab, the latter decided that after three years it was time to act. He probably derived confidence from his experience at the Battle of Karkar (or Qarqar) earlier the same year. He invited Jehoshaphat to join him in getting back the town, some fifty-five miles away across the River. It was perhaps a polite command, as the record suggests that Jehoshaphat was Ahab's vassal. Certainly they were related by marriage, for the King of Judah's son had wed Athaliah, Ahab's daughter, who was destined to be the only reigning queen that Judah or Israel ever had. The two monarchs in shining armour were sitting on thrones in the open in Samaria. Omri, Ahab's father, had moved his headquarters from Tirzah, having purchased the hill of Shemer (1,542 feet above sea-level). He had got it for a couple of silver talents – £850 according to the Moffatt translation and hence about £29,750 today – and named his new capital Samaria after the previous owner.[16]

Ahab consults Zedekiah and his 400 prophets, 'holy yes-men', who give the King the answer he wants: "Go up to Ramoth-gilead and prosper". The good Jehoshaphat is not convinced and wants a second opinion. Ahab admits that there is another seer, but complains that Michaiah son of Imlah is always a prophet of doom as far as he is concerned. Michaiah bravely spins a clever, if theologically dubious, yarn about God putting a lying spirit into the mouths of the court prophets to lure Ahab to his death. He pays for his honesty with incarceration and a diet of bread and water until the battle is over.

Ahab, taking no chances, disguises himself – yet he instructs Jehoshaphat to wear his royal robes in a mean attempt to 'draw fire' from himself. It doesn't work, because the thirty-two Syrian chariot captains recognised the King of Judah and they had orders to fight only against Ahab. "But one man drew his bow at random [literally, 'in his simplicity'] and hit the King of Israel where the breastplate joins the plates of armour." (I Kings 22:34) Ahab orders his driver to wheel round and take him out of the line. He watches the height of the battle propped up in his chariot, blood dripping on to its floor. The fighting ends with the death of Ahab and sunset. It seems that ancient armies were liable to panic, of which the decease of a

---

[16] The political and military importance of Omri and his son are greater than the Bible would suggest. Although the former reigned only 885–873 B.C., the Assyrian records call Israel 'The Land of Omri' for 150 years. Ahab sent 10,000 footmen and 2,000 chariots in a confederacy of twelve kings against Shalmaneser III at the Battle of Karkar (on the Orontes, some 230 miles north of Samaria) earlier in 853. His contingent was nearly one-fifth of the infantry and more than half the chariots. The allies suffered heavily, but appear to have halted the Assyrian king. Both Hebrew monarchs illustrate that the Scriptures are concerned principally with matters religious.

king or general was sufficient cause. Compare the effect on the enemy when Sisera was assassinated by Jael or when Judith beheads Holofernes at their private dinner. At any rate, the battle was apparently a draw – for everyone is sent home!

The old versions have "And a certain man drew a/his bow at a venture" and the saying has become proverbial. Brewer, in *Phrase and Fable*, defines it as "To attack without proper aim; to make a random remark which may hit the truth." There is another saying, or rather a mild expletive, which presumably comes from this story. 'Jumping Jehoshaphat!' dates from 1857 in the U.S.A.

Joram

852–841 B.C. (Israel)

Ahab is followed by his son Ahaziah who dies a year or two later after a fall from his window. Childless, he was succeeded by his brother Joram.

There is yet another coupling of sword and bow. Elisha has now taken on the mantle of Elijah his master – from which event the saying is derived – as the leading prophet in Israel. During a series of intended military engagements, the King of Syria (presumably Ben-hadad) is extremely put out when his plans become known to Joram. He is assured by his officers that it is not treachery, but Elisha's gift of clairvoyance. He therefore surrounds the prophet at Dothan with a considerable detachment of chariots by night in an attempt to kidnap him. Unknown to them, there is an even larger squadron of 'chariots of fire' on the neighbouring hills ... At Elisha's prayer, the soldiers are temporarily blinded and led by the prophet ten miles south to Samaria, the capital. The delighted King asks permission to slaughter the captured enemy. The Septuagint, followed now by the R.E.B., has the reading which is more likely to be the correct response: "Would you cut down prisoners you never captured with your own sword and bow?" (II Kings 6:22) Not only does Elisha's direction to Joram presage International Law, but also foreshadows the Divine Prophet's teaching about revenge and doing good to enemies. Not content with merely forbidding a massacre, he makes the King feed the Syrians before sending them home. Joram does more: he feasts them. He is rewarded, for there is no more raiding for the time being.

Jehu
841–813 B.C. (Israel)[17]

The event which led to his accession is illustrated by the late Nicholas Ford.[18] It is a graphic story and it demonstrates the point that such narratives cannot always be appreciated unless close attention is paid to the text and a map is used.

A decade after Ahab, Jehoram was mortally wounded by an archer. This time it was deliberate assassination by Jehu and not a stray shot. He reminds one rather of Oliver Cromwell (A.D. 1599–1658) in our fourteen-year Commonwealth period – a general who turned head of state, with a reforming zeal and a degree of ruthlessness, carried to extremes in the ninth-century case.

Jehu was in council with his commanders at Ramoth-gilead, which Ahab had failed to re-capture, during war with Syria. In

---

[17] The year 841 is an important date for chronology. The Assyrian black obelisk in the British Museum implies that Jehu paid tribute then to Shalmaneser III, although he may have acceded a year or more earlier.
[18] The picture is an artist's impression and it is appreciated that the bow-type is incorrect for the period. Ford died in his twenties.

comes a young prophet sent by Elisha, who in private pours oil over Jehu's head – the only instance of a northern monarch being anointed. Minutes later, to the sound of a trumpet, his brother officers gladly proclaim him king on a carpet of their cloaks. He drives swiftly in his chariot the forty-five miles due westwards over the Jordan to Jezreel, a ride which in 1682 gave a new word – 'Jehu' – to the English language for a cab-driver!

Ironically, King Joram was recovering from an engagement on his own soil with Hazael, King of Syria. Again the Greek LXX is of more interest than the Hebrew: "Joram, King of Isreal, was being cured in Jezreel from the arrows with which the Syrians had shot him down in Rama." (IV Kings 9:16) He got up from a sick bed and into his chariot to learn the news of Ramoth-gilead from his Commander-in-Chief. They meet in the vineyard that his mother Jezebel had got for Ahab from the judicially murdered Naboth. After a brief verbal exchange, Jehoram wheels round to escape, but "Jehu seized his bow and shot Jehoram between the shoulders; the arrow pierced his heart and he sank down in his chariot." (II Kings 9:24)

King Ahaziah of Judah, who had been sick-visiting, started to flee in his chariot when he had heard his ally's "Treachery, Ahaziah!" and saw what had happened. There then began a nine-mile chase to Ibleam. According to the Syriac and Latin versions: "Jehu pursued him and said, 'Shoot him also'; and they shot him in the chariot." (verse 27) Unlike Joram, the southern monarch evidently had a driver, for he reached Megiddo (some twelve miles to the north-west) where he died of his wounds. The first of these two shots is unique in the Bible, in that not only was the victim a moving target, but the archer may have been mobile too.

Jehu shooting at Joram; Ahaziah temporarily escapes.

Jehoash

798–782 B.C. (Israel)

There are two further incidents, both of them unique and fascinating, connected with Elisha. A vivid picture is given, portrayed on the cover by Sir Frank Dicksee, of the last recorded utterance of the aged prophet early in the eighth century when there was still strife between Israel and Syria.

Seeing the sick old man on his death-bed, King Jehoash (also called Joash) weeps over him: "My father, my father, you are worth chariots and horsemen to Israel!" There then follow two examples of what some might call 'sympathetic magic', but the present writer feels that the term 'prophetic symbolism' is to be preferred. " 'Take bow and arrows', said Elisha, and he took bow and arrows. 'Put your hand to the bow', said the prophet. He did so, and Elisha laid his hands on those of the King. Then he said, 'Open the window toward the east'; he opened it and Elisha told him to shoot, and he shot. Then the prophet said, 'An arrow for the Lord's victory, an arrow for victory over Syria! You will defeat Syria utterly at Aphek'." (II Kings 13:14–17)

Which Aphek? Clearly not the one in Asher in the north. The Aphek in I Kings 20:16 may well have been in the Plain of Sharon in Ephraim. However, it seems obvious that the one alluded to here is on the far side of the River, near what was later called the Sea of Galilee, partly because Jehoash was directed to shoot (north-) east and partly because the Syrians occupied Trans-Jordan.

Elisha had requested a double share of Elijah's spirit just before the latter's ascension (II Kings 2). Similarly, but on a lesser scale, Elisha hoped to communicate something of his power to Jehoash, laying his hand on his sovereign's when he was holding the weapon. Does the Bible mean that Elisha had one hand on the King's bow-hand and the other on his arrow-hand, as if teaching a young beginner? If so, the instruction about the window is out of place. This point has been missed in at least three twentieth-century translations which imply that Jehoash opened the casement when at full draw!

Another comic point is worth noting. Whereas the normal text in the LXX has the usual Greek word for 'shoot-an-arrow' (*toxeuo*), one version has an onomatopoeic verb – evidently a colloquialism – which is roughly translated " 'Whizz!' – and he whizzed."

Immediately comes a sequel which perhaps surprised Jehoash. "'Now take up your arrows.' When the King had taken them, Elisha said, 'Strike the ground with them.' He struck three times and stopped. The man of God was furious with him and said, 'You should have struck five or six times; then you would have defeated Syria utterly; as it is, you will strike Syria three times and no more.' Then Elisha died and was buried." (II Kings 13:18–20) The second symbolic act is harder to interpret. Maybe Elisha expected Jehoash to go on hitting the ground until instructed to cease. Perhaps he sensed that the King, now assured of victory, was half-heartedly humouring him and the prophet saw in this a defect of character.

Uzziah (Azariah)

767–740 B.C. (Judah)

This is the monarch whose death dates Isaiah's famous vision (6:1–8) to the year 740 and which inspired the well-known hymn 'Bright the vision that delighted once the sight of Judah's seer.' He has a very brief biography of nine verses in II Kings, where he is called Azariah. Fortunately, the chronicler had access to a history compiled by Isaiah (not the present prophetical book). The author, producing nearly four times as much, indicates that Uzziah was a much more important ruler than the Book of Kings implies, and this is apparently supported by archaeological evidence. Indeed, Professor Jacob M. Myers, writing about the Books of Chronicles as a whole, states that "... archaeological and historical studies have now rendered it (i.e., the work of the Chronicler) more respectable and have shown it to be at times more accurate than some of its parallel sources."[19]

There is a passing reference to the preparation of bows and stones for slinging, along with shields, spears, helmets, and coats of mail. What is intriguing is the next verse, although concerned with arrows only and not with real archery: "In Jerusalem he [Uzziah] made machines, invented by skilful men, to be on the towers and the corners, to discharge arrows and large stones." (II Chronicles 26:14–15)

According to Sir Ralph Payne-Gallwey in *Projectile-Throwing Engines of The Ancients* (1907) p. 5, this is the earliest allusion to such a weapon – none being depicted on the bronze doors of King Shalmaneser III of Assyria (858–824 B.C.) in the British Museum. It seems that the ballista is not found elsewhere until the expedition of Dionysius of Syracuse against the Carthaginians in 397 B.C.

As the Chronicler compiled his books – which include Ezra and Nehemiah – about 300 B.C., one can imagine some scholars maintaining that the writer was ascribing the 'sophisticated' catapults of his own day to an age 450 years earlier. (Four centuries later, according to Josephus, an engine projected a 58 lb. weight

---

[19] J. M. Myers, *I and II Chronicles* (Introduction to 2nd Edition, 1974) in the *Anchor Bible Commentary* series. I am grateful to the Rector of St John's Seminary, near Guildford, for admission to the Library on this and several previous occasions.

over 400 yards – about 365 metres – at the Siege of Jerusalem in
A.D. 70.) In fact scepticism about these machines has been voiced
by Professor Myers, who was referred to above. Going on the
analogy of the defences at Lachish, which had been fortified by
Solomon's son Rehoboam, he maintains that the word in question means some sort of protective battlement from which to
discharge missiles and that ballistas had not then been invented.
The latter argument is, of course, begging the question! There
may well have been some prototype, a kind of crossbow on a
frame perhaps. Maybe it was crude and not very effective and
there was a gap of four and a half centuries before it was tried
again more successfully. At all events, the New English Bible,
the Jerusalem Bible, the New International Version, the Revised
Standard Version, and Moffatt saw no reason to doubt the traditional rendering and neither does the Revised English Bible.
Contrary to two previous occasions, however, the *New* Jerusalem Bible deprives us of a text by playing safe: "He also erected
expertly contrived devices for the towers and angles of Jerusalem
from which to shoot arrows and drop large stones." Evidently
the translator gave in to the scruples of archaeologists, for a
footnote is appended: "Defensive screens projecting from the
stonework, not platforms for catapults which were still unknown at that epoch." The only gain is that the 1966 version had
contained the solecism 'to fire' arrows.

Hezekiah

715–687 B.C. (Judah)

Israel is no more. After a rebellion by the last King, Hoshea,
Shalmaneser V of Assyria (now Iraq) began the three-year Siege
of Samaria, which fell to his son Sargon II in 721. There followed
an exchange of populations: settlers were brought in from Baby-

Two iron arrowheads from the Siege of Lachish in 701 – the time of King Hezekiah. Note that the tips have been bent over from striking the town walls. Again, they are not necessarily the arrowheads of the attacking Assyrians, for they could be Hebrew ones shot back at the defenders by the Assyrians. (Courtesy, The Manchester Museum.)

Ionia and Syria (the origin of the Samaritans), while Israelites from northern and central Palestine were deported to Assyria. Sargon records little more than 27,000 being taken, so the 'Ten Lost Tribes' is largely a myth. In 701

> The Assyrian came down like a wolf on the fold,
> And his cohorts were gleaming in purple and gold ...

– so wrote Byron in 1815 in his poem 'The Destruction of Sennacherib'. Sennacherib had succeeded his father Sargon three years before, but had to spend the beginning of his reign suppressing a series of rebellions. Sennacherib, having taken a year to crush Babylon, sweeps westwards through Syria to Phoenicia, and south to Philistia. After defeating an Egyptian army that came to assist, he turns to deal with Judah which now stands alone. He captured Lachish, mentioned earlier, about ten leagues south-west of Jerusalem, setting up his headquarters there. The siege is vividly, and in parts horribly, portrayed on bas-reliefs in his palace at

Nineveh, the capital. He boasts, according to the 'Prism' of Sennacherib, that he reduced forty-six of the cities of Judah, shutting up Hezekiah in Jerusalem 'like a bird in a cage'. He imposed a penalty for revolting of thirty talents of gold and 300 silver ones, augmented by another 500 probably from the captured towns.

After the King of Judah has received a threatening message from Assyrian envoys, he goes in sackcloth to the Temple and sends a delegation of two members of his government and senior priests to the great statesman-prophet Isaiah, requesting his prayers. Isaiah was sympathetic to Hezekiah for he appears to have been a good ruler who instituted a mini-reformation which perhaps paved the way for Josiah's. At any rate, Isaiah has words of reassurance that Sennacherib would hear a rumour and return to Assyria and there be assassinated. This happened, but not till 680 when two of his sons killed the King at worship in Nineveh.

Before this occurred, it seems that Sennacherib invaded Judah again in about 690 – unless the two accounts are parallel narratives, which Isaiah's age might suggest. Hezekiah receives a letter from the Assyrian monarch asking why he supposes that his God would deliver him, listing nine nations – some of them city-states perhaps – whose gods had let them down. The King goes again into the Temple and spreads out the letter before the Lord (something which the present writer has done on one or two momentous occasions) and earnestly prays. He is assured once more by the prophet, who must now be in his seventies at least since he began his ministry in about 740, that his supplication has been heard. "Therefore thus says the Lord concerning the King of Assyria: 'He shall not come into this City or shoot an arrow there, or come before it with a shield or cast up a siege mound against it'." (II Kings 19:32) This was more than a figure of speech, since the Assyrian method of attacking a fortified town, as shown on many reliefs, included the planting of huge shields or screens from behind which showers of arrows were poured against the defenders on the battlements. There is confirmation that *belos*, the generic word for a missile, certainly can mean 'arrow' in the Greek Old Testament: *kai ou toxeusei ekei belos* – "and he shall not shoot there an arrow".

The Assyrian army? According to the Bible, 185,000 soldiers perished overnight. One theory is that it was bubonic plague (associated with mice); another, that it was malignant malaria which can kill quickly. The mouse element comes in the secular historian Herodotus, regarding the deliverance of Egypt from Sennacherib: field mice ate the enemy quivers, bowstrings, and the leather handles of shields (2:141).

Josiah
639–608 B.C. (Judah)

According to the second-century writer of Ecclesiasticus, one of the most important books in the Apocrypha, David, Hezekiah and Josiah (who began his reign at eight) were the only good kings that Judah ever had. "The memorial of Josiah is like the composition of incense prepared by the work of the apothecary: it shall be sweet as honey in every mouth, and as music at the banquet of wine. He behaved himself uprightly in the conversion of the people, and took away the abominations of iniquity. He set his heart right toward the Lord; in the days of wicked men, he made godliness to prevail." (49:1–3)

It was not a question of personal morality or good government but religion, the operative word in the eulogy being 'conversion'. It relates to the Reformation which he inaugurated in 621 B.C., sparked off by the discovery of the Book of the Law during repairs to the Temple. The High Priest and the Secretary of State went with three other officials to consult Huldah, one of four prophetesses in the Old Testament. As a result, the 'high places' were abolished and worship was centralised at Jerusalem. It is

almost certain that this Book of the Law was none other than
the middle part of our Deuteronomy – which means 'Second Law'
(II Kings 22 and 23). Thirteen years later King Josiah intercepts
Pharaoh Necho II of Egypt at Megiddo (Armageddon), some
twenty-two miles north of Samaria. A tablet which was discovered this century and a remark by the Jewish historian Josephus
make it clear that the King of Egypt was going in support of the
last sovereign of the dying Assyrian Empire. Nineveh had fallen
in 612 B.C. as a result of the alliance of Babylonians, Medes and
Scythians. The Book of Nahum – "Woe to the bloody city!" –
is a song of triumph over the end of a cruel regime. The final
collapse was at the Battle of Haran (400 miles from Jerusalem)
in 609 – later called Carrhae, where a Roman army under Crassus
succumbed to massed Parthian arrows in 53 B.C.

What is not plain in Kings is why Josiah went to meet Pharaoh.
Chronicles gives a fuller account from which one can deduce that
Josiah himself took the initiative; that is, he was not summoned.
Perhaps he wanted to stop the Egypto-Assyrian alliance; perhaps
he had an eye to gaining some territory in what had been Israel.
The Chronicler states that Pharaoh remonstrated via envoys with
the King of Judah that he had no quarrel with him and that he
(Josiah) must not stand in God's way or *He* (sic) would destroy
him. Josiah would not listen, however, and in battle in the plain of
Megiddo "the archers shot King Josiah" in his chariot. (II Chronicles 35:23) He was taken in another chariot the sixty miles to
Jerusalem where he died at thirty-nine years of age – a tragic loss
to the nation.[20] Although two decades were to elapse before the

---

[20] Jeremiah, who must have welcomed the Reformation, surprisingly discour-
ages mourning for Josiah. "Weep not for the dead nor brood over his loss.
Weep rather for him who has gone away, for he shall never return, never again
see the land of his birth." (22:10) The latter remark refers to the eighteen-year-
old Jehoahaz who was deposed by Pharaoh after a three-month reign and sent
captive to Egypt. Necho himself was defeated at the Battle of Carchemish on

Fall of Jerusalem and the Exile, it was the beginning of the end of the southern kingdom.

Nehemiah

444 B.C.

As Hoshea of Israel had rebelled against the Assyrian overlord, so Jehoiachin revolted against Babylon. King Nebuchadnezzar, after capturing Jerusalem, sent Judah into Exile, which is sometimes called the Captivity, in two main deportations. One was with the eighteen-year-old King Jehoiachin, after a reign of only three months, in 597 when the cream of the nation was taken. He was succeeded by his young uncle Zedekiah who rebelled also and this led to a second deportation in 586. There was a small third one five years later involving some 800 people, which only Jeremiah mentions.

In 539 Cyrus the Great, the first King of Persia, conquered Babylon. The next year he released the Jews, along with other nations, to their homeland. Almost a century later Nehemiah, Cupbearer to Artaxerxes I at the fortress of Susa, learns from his brother that Jerusalem has had its walls broken down, evidently from a raid implied in the Book of Ezra, and is generally in trouble. The King notices his sad countenance when Nehemiah is on duty and enquires what he was worried about. After the explanation, Artaxerxes asks what he wants. Nehemiah makes an instant petition to God and immediately replies to the King. This may well be the earliest example of what is known as an 'arrow

---

the Euphrates (only a hundred miles east of the Mediterranean coast) in 605. The Egyptians by treaty relinquished any foothold in Asia and for three centuries ceased to be a great power.

prayer'! (Nehemiah 2:4–5) As a consequence, Nehemiah becomes Governor of Judah.

His task was not only reconstruction, but having to defend the City from the jealous semi-heathen Samaritans, under their leaders, Sanballat – who became Governor of Samaria forty years on – and Tobiah, a descendant of the Ammonites found in the early books of the Bible. The traditional weapons have now been joined by a third: "Accordingly, I posted my people by families armed with swords, spears and bows ..." After surveying the position, Nehemiah encourages nobles, magistrates and people not to be afraid; to remember the Lord; and to fight for their families and homes. He mentions that the enemy realized that everything was known and that God had frustrated their plans. After saying that they all returned to work on the wall, his memoirs continue: "From that day forward half the men under me were engaged in the actual building, while the other half stood by holding their spears, shields, and bows, and wearing coats of mail." (Nehemiah 4:13 and 16) The second reference probably alludes to his Persian guard of officers and cavalry.

Nehemiah may seem to us smug and self-satisfied at times, but he was a pious man who did a good job. He entertained 150 at his table, despite refusing the Governor's allowance during his twelve years in office. "Also of Nehemiah the memorial is great; who raised up for us the walls that were fallen, and set up the gates and bars, and raised up our homes again." (Ecclesiasticus 49:13)

The Prophets

There are references in half-a-dozen of the prophetical books, ranging from Amos in the middle of the eighth century to Second Zechariah after the Exile. There is a small problem in classification. Generally it is clear whether any writer in the Old Testament is speaking about the bow and arrow literally or metaphorically; a separate section will deal with the latter category. However, there are a number of allusions in the prophets which are difficult to classify. Many should really be thought of as semi-metaphorical, but it would be unpractical and often arbitrary to place them in a third group. As with the historical books, an attempt will be made to put the texts into some sort of chronological order.

Amos

The Book of Amos is probably the oldest in the Bible – not the oldest piece of writing, as was seen in connection with Judges 5 which is twelfth-century. The prophet was a shepherd and dresser of sycamore trees in Tekoa of Judah but preached in Israel, starting his ministry about 760 B.C. – seven years before the traditional date for the founding of Rome. Amos opens with two chapters of denunciations on eight nations, including his own Judah, ending with Israel itself. After castigating the northern kingdom, he predicts God's vengeance when "he who handles the bow shall not stand." (2:15)

Hosea

Roughly contemporary with Amos was Hosea, a true northerner, who stressed God's love as Amos had emphasised His justice. Unlike Elisha and the editors of the Books of Kings, Hosea disapproves of Jehu's massacre of the House of Ahab: "I will punish the line of Jehu for the blood shed in Jezreel and put an end to the Kingdom of Israel. On that day I will break Israel's bow in the Vale of Jezreel." (1:4–5) Jezreel (Esdraelon) was the traditional battle-ground in the north and the prophet's words were at least partially fulfilled when it fell into Assyrian hands in 733, a decade before the final overthrow of the northern kingdom. It is interesting that 'bow' is used to signify arms, even if by a type of synecdoche. Professor W. E. Barnes, D.D., commenting on the story of the dying Elisha and the King and citing this passage, goes so far as to say that "the bow was the national weapon."[21] Whether this is so or not, Amos also mentions the bow only.

The second passage in Hosea, two verses on, is rather different. It alludes to the southern kingdom: "Then I will love Judah and will save them. I will save them not by bow or sword or weapon of war ..." (1:7) The N.E.B. regards it as an interpolation and banishes the verse to a footnote; the R.E.B. has restored it! N.J.B. speculates that the verse was added by Hosea's disciples after the Fall of Samaria when they had taken refuge in Judah. It may well refer to the deliverance of Judah at the end of the eighth century when, as stated earlier, 185,000 Assyrians are said to have perished without a blow being struck.

Finally, looking forward to a time of permanent peace, Hosea declares: "I will break bow and sword and weapon of war and sweep them off the earth ...." (2:18)

Isaiah

Next come several passages from the pen of Isaiah, who was mentioned briefly in the story of Hezekiah. His long ministry began in about 740 and lasted at least until 701 and maybe into the next century. Anthropomorphically, he pictures God hoisting a signal and whistling to the distant Assyrians to come and act as His agents of chastisement, whose "arrows are sharpened and their bows all strung." (5:28)

Hunting with the bow is rarely mentioned. There is an allusion in the context of power politics: Pekah of Israel and Rezin of Syria in 735 try to force Ahaz of Judah to join the general alliance against Assyria's expansionism. (Ashurbanipal in 663

---

21 *Cambridge Bible for Schools and Colleges, II Kings* (1928), p. 65.

was to capture Thebes in Egypt – the No-amon of Nahum 3:8.)
King Ahaz appeals to Assyria, becoming its vassal in consequence. Isaiah strongly disapproved of such faithlessness and
warns, among other things, that the land once rich in vines would
be taken over by thorns and briars. "A man shall go there only
to hunt with bow and arrows." (7:24) As far as the northern
kingdom was concerned, Tiglath-Pileser III (Pul) in 734 deported
the inhabitants of half-a-dozen towns in Naphtali, north of Galilee, and, according to I Chronicles 5:26, the three Trans-Jordan
tribes as well in 733–732, Damascus falling in the latter year. It
was an earnest of what was to happen to the rest of Israel a dozen
years later.

The next oracle, on Babylon, probably dates from the 550s and
so cannot be by Isaiah himself.[22] It proclaims that the bows of
the Medes shall dash the young Babylonians to the ground. (13:18)
The N.E.B. and R.E.B. have the archery text as a footnote. The
passages relating to Kedar in chapter 21 were dealt with in the
section on Genesis.

There are two mentions in the Valley of Vision, Isaiah's bitter-
est prophecy. The year is 701 B.C. when, as was noted before,
Sennacherib of Assyria had been at the gates of Jerusalem. Previously Isaiah's tone was one of encouragement, but it seems that
he is looking now with stern disapproval at the mood of the
capital after King Hezekiah had bought off Sennacherib who
then raised the siege – only temporarily, it would appear. According to the N.E.B. translators, this is a rare example of a
'bowshot': "Your commanders are all in flight, huddled together
out of bowshot." (22:3). There may have been a liberty taken
here, however, for the literal meaning is "from the bow they are

---

[22] It must originate long after Isaiah, for the Babylonian Empire did not exist
in his time; the Jews are in exile which was in the sixth century; and it was to
be the Persians – supported, it is true, by the Medes – who conquered Babylon.

imprisoned". The R.E.B. is more cautious perhaps with 'fleeing in groups from the bow'. The prophet mentions that the enemy had Elamite archers, from the south-east of Assyria, as allies: "Elam took up his quiver." (22:6)

Isaiah 37:33 is parallel to II Kings 19:32 and has already been dealt with.

Jeremiah

There are more than a dozen pasages in Jeremiah and a brief introduction is necessary. The prophet came of a priestly family from Anathoth in Benjamin, four miles north of Jerusalem. He prophesied in the reigns of five kings, from Josiah to Zedekiah, 626–586 B.C. In the latter period of his ministry he had the unenviable task of proclaiming that it was actually God's Will that the southern kingdom should surrender to the Babylonians – at best a defeatist; at worst a traitor. He was in a sense a kind of Cassandra at Troy and, like the beautiful royal prophetess, he was right. Jeremiah was one of the greatest saints of the Old Testament and has even been put forward as a possible 'original' for the Suffering Servant poems in the Book of Isaiah (written by Baruch?), fulfilled, Christians believe, six centuries later. Jeremiah unwillingly escaped to Egypt in about 581, after the Governor's assassination, in a party which included his secretary Baruch – the remains of whose house have been found and his seal – and the young daughters of the captured King Zedekiah. According to 'British Israelite' theory, the British Monarchy can be traced back to King David via one of these royals.

Early in his ministry, the prophet predicts disaster coming from the mysterious north. "At the sound of the horsemen and archers the whole country is in flight." (4:29) There were invasions of Scythians from north of the Crimea in about 625, who got as far as Askelon (formerly one of the five Philistine towns) on their way to Egypt. Jeremiah may well have had these hordes in mind as Yahweh's agents of punishment.

On the other hand, the next two passages probably relate to Assyria before the Fall of Nineveh in 612. "Their quiver is an open sepulchre" (5:16) cannot refer to the Scythians. They might be described as distant and mighty, but not as an ancient nation (verse 15). The quiver being described as an open sepulchre is a good example of the semi-metaphor – a figure of speech with a literal meaning too. The New English Bible, followed by the Revised English Bible, accepts the Syriac reading: "Their jaws are a grave, wide open", giving an image of human locusts in verse 17. The northern invaders "lay hold on bow and scimitar; they are cruel and have no mercy" (6:23), a delineation which fits Assyria all too well. What Jeremiah is saying is that what Sargon did to the northern kingdom in the previous century, one of his successors could do to them if they do not repent.

The prophet, maybe not Jeremiah himself in chapters 46 to 51, pictures Pharoah Necho of Egypt addressing his troops before the ill-fated Battle of Carchemish on the Euphrates in 605.[23] Among his allies are 'Lydians grasping their bent bows' (46:9) from western Asia Minor.

As already stated, the exile was brought about by two main deportations of the Jews to Babylon in 597 and 586. Early in the reign of Zedekiah, the last King of Judah who ruled as a puppet in the eleven-year gap, an oracle promised that the Lord would "break the bow of Elam, the chief weapon of their might." (49:35)

---

[23] The discovery of four tablets in 1956 indicates that the Egyptian army was totally annihilated – which excavations had already hinted at. The greater surprise is that it was apparently rebuilt in four years, well enough heavily to defeat Nebuchadnezzar in 601. This may have given confidence to Jehoiakim of Judah to rebel against him in 598 – but it was his eighteen-year-old son Jehoiachin who paid for it by virtual life imprisonment (II Kings 24:8 and 25:27–30).

In other words, the prophet was trying to comfort those left behind that the allies of their Babylonian conquerors would be crushed in due course. They came from the east of Babylon, north of the Persian Gulf. The Elamite quiver was previously mentioned in Isaiah 22:6. The oracles in chapters 50 and 51 relate to the downfall of Babylon. Although they may reflect much of Jeremiah's teaching, scholars are almost unanimous that they cannot come as they stand from the prophet himself, for three or four reasons. It will be convenient to take the texts as a whole, since they all have the same theme. With one possible exception, all refer to the enemies of the super power. "I shall stir up a host of mighty nations [Herodotus says that there were twenty-two] … Their arrows are like those of a skilled warrior who never returns empty-handed." (50:9)

"Marshal your forces against Babylon, on every side, you whose bows are ready strung; shoot at her, spare no arrows." (50:14). "Let your arrows be heard whistling against Babylon, all you whose bows are ready strung." (50:29) The allusion in verse 42 of the same chapter relating to Babylon is simply a repeat of 6:23 which referred to Assyria. It illustrates the point that these two chapters draw extensively from other prophets and from the rest of Jeremiah.

The next reference is obscure. It is not clear whether the archer is being urged to attack Babylon, "Let the archer bend his bow" (so Moffatt); or, alluding to the Babylonian defender, "How shall the archer then string his bow?" (N.E.B.); or is it archer v. archer? "Against him that bends, let the archer bend his bow." (R.V., margin) (51:3) The prophet declares: "Sharpen the arrows, fill the quivers. The Lord has roused the spirit of the king[s] of the Medes." (51:11) The N.E.B. translates *shelet* as 'quiver' (as it did at II Samuel 8:7), which makes more sense than 'fill the shields'.

Lastly the prophet pictures the final scene of the Fall of Babylon, which was to occur in 539 B.C. "For marauders march on Babylon herself, her warriors are captured and their bows are broken." (51:56)

Ezekiel

Next the baffling but interesting Book of Ezekiel, which the Jews apparently were not allowed to read until they were thirty! The only prophet who was also a priest (though Jeremiah did come of a priestly family), he worked for at least twenty-two years in the sixth century among the exiles in Babylon, some 700 miles east of Jerusalem. Although Ezekiel overlapped a decade with Jeremiah, he really began where the latter left off. The book contains a couple of unique references: the casting of lots, and firewood. The prophet, perhaps in one of his trances, pictures King Nebuchadnezzar in the future halting at the parting of the roads – perhaps at Damascus – on his way southwards in about 588. He is undecided whether to turn left for Rabbath, the Ammonite capital on the east of Jordan, or right for Jerusalem. Accordingly, he will consult the teraphim or household gods, inspect livers (probably of sheep) and 'will shake the arrows' (21:21). Presumably one shaft was inscribed with a J and the other with an R, both arrows perhaps being shaken up in a quiver. To the King's right hand will come the lot against Jerusalem (verse 22) – and two years later the capital falls. According to G. A. Cooke in the International Critical Commentary, this kind of divination is common practice among Arabs.

There are a couple of allusions in the mysterious narratives about Gog and Magog, statues of whom are familiar at The Guildhall in the City of London. The original ones were carved by Captain Richard Saunders in 1708, but were destroyed in the 'blitz' of December 1940 during the Second World War. The present statues were fashioned by David Evans and were installed in June 1953.[24]

---

[24] I am indebted to Mr. M. V. Roberts (a fellow member of The Worshipful Company of Fletchers), Deputy Librarian at Guildhall Library, for this information.

Statue of Gog at Guildhall, London, from 1708 until its destruction in 1940.
(Courtesy, Guildhall Library, City of London)

After a period of peace – to return to Ezekiel – the prophet describes a gigantic alliance of heathen hordes from the far north who launch a final assault on the people of God. Gog (darkness?) was the Commander-in-Chief. 'Magog' here appears to signify his domain; in three passages outside Ezekiel he is a person. All is well, however, for Yahweh promises Gog that He "will strike the bow from your left hand and dash the arrows from your right hand." Because of the Guildhall figure, one pictures a giant on foot – Goliath as a bowman. It is probable, however, that Gog represents the Scythian horsed archers from the north who reached the frontier of Egypt in 630–625 and who will come again ...

The slaughter of the hordes will be so great that it will take seven months to bury the corpses on the east of the Dead Sea. "The dwellers in the cities of Israel [sic] shall come out and gather weapons to light their fires, bucklers and shields, bows and arrows, throwing-sticks and lances, and they shall kindle fires with them for seven years." (39:3 and 9). Archery tackle as firewood actually happened a century and a half later during the march of the 'Ten Thousand' in 400 B.C. The retreating Greeks used the arrows of Persian deserters for fuel. (Xenophon's *Anabasis* 2:1:6)

Second Isaiah

Probably two decades after the close of Ezekiel's ministry, the next mention comes from the pen of so-called Deutero- or Second Isaiah or Isaiah of Babylon (chapters 40–55). He was the great unknown Prophet of the Exile who makes monotheism explicit. For reasons of historical background, theology, and language, scholars have held since the last century that the author was not Isaiah of Jerusalem.

Cyrus, the founder of the Persian Empire which was to last two centuries till Alexander the Great, had conquered Media in 550 and in 546 overthrew Croesus, the last King of Lydia who was proverbial for riches. Around that year, the prophet claims that God has raised up this man from the east – even naming him and calling him His 'anointed' – and has given him the power to subdue kings. "He scatters them with his sword like dust and with his bow like chaff before the wind." (41:2) Note the sword-and-bow combination. Cyrus entered Babylon in 539 without opposition and released the Jews the following year after a 'captivity' of half-a-century.

Third Isaiah

There appears to be a reference in the post-exilic Trito- or Third Isaiah (chapters 56–66) at 66:19, alluding to the Lydians 'who draw the bow'. However, the text is doubtful. N.E.B. and R.E.B. substitute two further place-names, putting the alleged archery text in a footnote. N.J.B. has a helpful note on the six places.

Second Zechariah

Finally, as far as the literal passages in the prophets are concerned, come two texts in so-called Second Zechariah. Zechariah himself was a contemporary of Haggai in 520 after the Exile, but chapters 9–11 and 12–14 are believed possibly to date to the next century. The late Dr Lowther Clarke, Canon Residentiary of Chichester Cathedral in West Sussex, in his Commentary described these six chapters as 'the hardest in the Old Testament' – an opinion shared in Gore (see Bibliography). Two references with the description 'battle-bow' are not found elsewhere, which suggests the same author for both sections. However, they look as if they were written at different periods, for one speaks of peace while the other is bellicose: "They shall produce men to be supports and stays, men to be battle-bows and rulers." (10:4) The context is a hoped-for return from Egypt and 'Assyria'. The other one, by contrast, is in the famous prophecy fulfilled by Jesus on Palm Sunday: "Rejoice ... your king is coming to you

... humble and mounted on an ass ... he shall banish chariots from Ephraim [sic] and war-horses from Jerusalem and the battle-bow". (9:9–10) 'Sic', because Ephraim – that is, Israel in the north and centre – had fallen more than two centuries earlier. Similarly, the emphatic 'sic' was inserted in connection with Ezekiel 39:9.

The Apocrypha

'Apocrypha' is a Greek neuter plural, meaning 'hidden (things)' – from which are derived crypt and cryptic. It is a collection of fifteen books, mostly in Greek, which originated among the Jews in Egypt. As probably less than five per cent of Bibles contain the collection, which was only made a separate unit in A.D. 1520, a short introduction has been added as another appendix. There are a dozen references, half of them figurative which will be dealt with later.

About the year 165 B.C., Judas Maccabaeus, the hero cele-brated by Handel in the Oratorio of that name, is threatened by a massive counter-attack by Timotheus, whose base is beyond the Jordan. Judas led out his army, presumably north-eastwards from Jerusalem, to meet the mercenaries and 'Asian' cavalry of the Ammonite commander who hoped to conquer Judaea. "As the fighting grew hot, the enemy saw in the sky five magnificent figures riding horses with golden bridles, who placed themselves at the head of the Jews, formed a circle round Maccabaeus, and kept him invulnerable under the protection of their armour. They launched arrows and thunderbolts at the enemy, who, confused and blinded, broke up in complete disorder." Whether or not it was a mass hallucination on the part of the enemy, 20,500 of their infantry and 600 cavalry were said to have perished, while Ti-motheus fled to his garrison at Gezer (II Maccabees 10:24–32).

The incident is strongly reminiscent of the 'Angels of Mons' story in World War I and is well worth a digression. The Battle of Mons was fought on 23rd August 1914, the first engagement of The Great War and Britain's first battle in Europe for ninety-nine years. The angels were said to have protected our retreating troops, whereupon General Von Kluck turned back from the pursuit. John A. Terraine in *The Smoke and the Fire* (1980) deals with the legend on pp. 17–19. He mentions that Brigadier-General John Charteris recorded in a letter of 5th September, a fortnight after the battle, that the story of the Angel (sic) of Mons, in white and on a white horse, with flaming sword, was going strongly through II Corps. Private Frank Richards wrote that if any angels were seen on the retirement from Le Cateau, three days after Mons, they were seen that night. Richards quotes a soldier observing a non-existent castle after four days of continuous marching, with practically no sleep, and a distinguished lieutenant-colonel and two fellow officers, all dog-tired, seeing squadrons of cavalry on either side of them for twenty minutes.[25]

---

[25] Although John Terraine puts such phenomena down to extreme fatigue, it is beyond belief that neither he in *Mons – the Retreat to Victory* (1960) nor David Ascoli in *The Mons Star* (1981) makes any allusion to the famous legend.

Arthur Machen in *The Bowmen and Other Legends of the War* (London, 1915) claims that he started the myth. In a long introduction he states that a story entitled 'The Bowmen', published in *The Evening News* of 29th September 1914 – was Michaelmas Day a coincidence? – snowballed in a quite outstanding progression into the legend. Machen maintained that the link was an article by an A. P. Sinnett in *The Occult Review* of the following May, in which he wrote of a 'row of shining beings'. Machen conjectured (his word) that 'shining' was the connection between his 'bowmen' and the popular rumour of 'angels'. Machen, in a postscript, is sceptical as to interviews by Nurse Phyllis Campbell with a Lancashire Fusilier (a Methodist) and a Royal Field Artilleryman who claimed to see St George, because of discrepancies and lack of details.

Ralph Shirley wrote a pamphlet entitled *The Angel Warriors at Mons*, undated but presumably penned in World War I. As Editor of *The Occult Review*, alluded to above, Shirley was naturally not a sceptic. He claims on p. 2 that "such stories had indeed been widely current in France at the time of the retreat from Mons – nearly a month before the appearance of Mr Machen's story." He goes on to quote a vivid experience of an anonymous lance-corporal as related

Returning to the second century B.C., there is a brief reference to enemy archers in the Battle of Alasa (ten miles north-west of Jerusalem) in 160. "The slingers and the archers went ahead of the main force." (I Maccabees 9:11) Judas Maccabaeus, the great hero of Jewish independence, with only 800 remaining supporters, is tragically defeated and slain by the Syrians who have 20,000 infantry and 2,000 cavalry – illustrating the proportion of foot-soldiers to horsemen, to be noticed again later.

Apart from a quiver rattling on a horse (Job 39:23), the only direct evidence of mounted bowmen is in the Book of Judith, which is what one might call a historical novel. It concerns a devout, beautiful, rich widow who delivers Israel by beheading the enemy Commander-in-Chief at a private dinner – similar to

---

to Nurse C. M. Wilson. E. G. Heath in *Archery – A Military History* (1980) mentions, on pp. 165–6, two such stories. One involved Staff Colonel Shepheard travelling from Hazebrouch to Wimereux, who saw 'thousands' of gloomy grey-hooded archers of Crecy.

To return to Arthur Machen, it is not clear when he actually composed his story, but we must not neglect the fact that the letter from Brigadier-General John Charteris *was written twenty-four days before Machen's article was published*. This, of course, backs up the quotation from Ralph Shirley.

There is a tradition that emanated from survivors of The East Yorkshire Regiment that German soldiers had been admitted to a casualty clearing station with flechette wounds. These resulted from the counter-offensive *after* Mons. It is possible that they were caused by mini-arrows dropped from aeroplanes before guns were used, yet it appears that the planes were grounded at the time owing to bad weather ... Mayhap the wounds were inflicted by a forerunner of Colonel Jack Churchill, D.S.O., M.C., who (when a captain) shot a German with a hunting arrow and a yew bow of probably 80 lb. at L'Epinette, near Bethune, in May 1940, just before Dunkirk. It was a pleasure to meet Colonel Churchill, now in his eighties, and subsequently to have a long telephone conversation with him.

(I am grateful to Colonel A. J. Leahy for twice lending me the Shirley pamphlet; to Mr Hugh D. Soar, Hon. Secretary of The British Long-Bow Society, for drawing my attention to Gerry Heath's book and for other help; and to Mr George Thorley, another member of the Society, for information regarding the East Yorkshires.)

Jael killing Sisera, as narrated in the Book of Judges. The King of Assyria had sent Holophernes on a punitive expedition against Cilicia (where St Paul came from; modern south-east Turkey), Syria, Palestine and Egypt – and many cities en route, including Midianites in the far south – all of whom had not supported him in a successful war against Arphaxad of Media. Holophernes is ordered to muster 120,000 infantry and 12,000 cavalry, who are later referred to as 'twelve thousand archers on horse-back' (Judith 2:5 and 15).

Twelve thousand horsed archers must be an exaggeration when one considers that the highly professional Parthians had 10,000 at the Battle of Carrhae (Haran) in northern Mesopotamia in 53 B.C. against the Roman army of Crassus. There were 1,200 Dahae mounted bowmen (Scythians beyond the Caspian) at the Battle of Magnesia, a Greek city in Asia Minor, in 190 B.C. and this seems a much more probable number.[26] It may be that 120,000 for the infantry was a likely figure and our author arbitrarily put the cavalry at 12,000 in the ten-to-one ratio favoured by the Greeks.[27]

In any case, one is not obliged to take the figures regarding archers too seriously in view of the historical blunders: The King of Babylon for Assyria; Arphaxad unknown; the River Hydaspes is in India; neither Assyria nor Babylon demanded 'earth and water' as symbols of submission; the period is set both before and after the Exile. Mayhap at least one howler is deliberate: for 'Assyria' (which had collapsed in 612) read 'Syria', in much the same way that 'Babylon' appears instead of 'Rome' in the Book of Revelation to get past the authorities. For this and other reasons the book is dated *circa* 150 B.C., but some consider that it might be as late as about 50.

---

[26] Plutarch's *Life of Crassus*, chapters 24 and 25; Livy 37:40.
[27] *Oxford Classical Dictionary*, p. 99, column 1.

Apart from the cavalry making a reconnaissance (Judith 7:6 and 7), we do not hear of them specifically again, but there is a unique allusion to archery in a prayer. Judith herself supplicates: "Thou seest the Assyrians assembled in their strength, proud of their horses and riders, boasting of the power of their infantry, and putting their faith in shield and javelin, bow and sling ...." (9:7)

Chapter II

The Bow and Arrow as a Figure of Speech

Officially the term figurative is used for this section as it covers both metaphor and simile, in the same way as lawyer includes barrister and solicitor. In practice, however, 'metaphorical' may sometimes be employed loosely for convenience.

England is a cricketing nation, so it is not surprising that expressions such as 'a good innings' and 'a sticky wicket' have crept into our language. The bow appears to have been the national weapon among the Hebrews, so it is understandable that the Bible has metaphors reflecting this. What is astonishing is the number. There are some 130 references to archery in general, about fifty of which are figures of speech. Of the latter, half are in the Psalms, a dozen in the Prophets, seven in the Apocrypha, while eight are found in various other books.

Part I

God Against Enemies

"In the beginning God ..." so says Genesis 1:1. It is fitting to start with the Almighty, especially as nearly half the allusions apply to Him. In Greek mythology the arrows of Apollo repre-

sent sudden or gentle death. Not so in the Old Testament. Yahweh, the Divine Archer, rather resembles Zeus with thunderbolts. Certainly flashes of lightning are equated with Yahweh's
arrows:

> The Lord shall appear above them,
> and his arrow shall flash like lightning.
>
> (Zechariah 9:14)

> He loosed his arrows, he sped them far and wide,
> he shot forth lightning shafts and sent them echoing.
>
> (II Samuel 22:15 = Psalm 18:14)

> The clouds poured water, the skies thundered,
> thy arrows flashed hither and thither.
>
> (Psalm 77:17)

The noun used is, apparently, a fuller form of the normal word
for arrow – compare our 'till' and 'until' – and is a poetical term
for the flashes of lightning.

> The bolts of his lightning shall fly straight on the mark, they
> shall leap upon the target as if his bow in the clouds were
> drawn in its full arc, and the artillery of his resentment shall
> let fly a fury of hail.
>
> (Wisdom 5:21–22)

Another one from the Psalms is a prayer for deliverance from
enemies:

> Shoot forth thy lightning flashes far and wide,
> and send thy arrows whistling.
>
> (R.E.B. 'humming') (144:6)

This seems to be a repeat of Psalm 18, just noticed, but which
came first? The answer must presumably be the latter, if it is
indeed Davidic. There appears to be a similar imprecation in
Psalm 58:7 —

When he [God] aims his arrows,
Let them be as though they were cut off.

and the Greek version has:

He shall bend his bow till they shall fail.

However, the Hebrew is corrupt. Moffatt, R.S.V., N.E.B. and
N.J.B. all refer to trodden or trampled grass instead of archery,
the latter inserting a footnote about it. Interestingly enough, the
revision of 1989 has reverted to 'arrows' – thus agreeing with the
Authorized (1611) and Revised (1885) Versions.

One highly poetic passage is in Habakkuk, where sun and
moon are so impressed with God's missiles that they stop in their
tracks:

The sun forgets to turn in his course,
and the moon stands still at her zenith,
at the gleam of thy speeding arrows
and the glance of thy flashing spear.

(Habakkuk 3:11)

The only example of long range is in the Apocrypha:

For strong is his arm which bends the bow, and sharp the arrows
which he shoots; once they are on their way, they will not stop
before they reach the ends of the earth.

(II Esdras 16:13)

The R.E.B. has changed it to 'nothing will stop them'. Although
a fruitless intervention against the shafts may well be what the
writer had in mind, it does not have the same meaning as the
earlier version. The latter could simply imply that God's arrows
will not 'run out of steam'.

Amid so many bellicose, or at any rate semi-warlike, passages
come two peaceful ones where God is the Anti-archer.

He has broken the flashing arrows [*lit.* 'the flames of the bow'],
shield and sword and weapons of war.

(Psalm 76:3)

The second is better known:

... from end to end of the earth he stamps out war:
be breaks the bow, he snaps the spear
and burns the shield [Hebrew 'chariots'] in the fire.

(Psalm 46:9)

Of course, God as an Archer is an anthropomorphism, but
there are several passages where this is especially marked. His
bow-case is implied by Habakkuk (*c.* 600 B.C. and so a contemporary of Jeremiah): "Thy bow was quite bared." (3:9) The force
of the 'quite' may be that it was always partially visible as in
ancient representations of our weapon, sometimes strung, in a
case. Indeed, both English Bibles speak of God drawing His bow
from its case. The New English Bible, following one version of
the Greek Old Testament, adds: "and charge thy quiver with
shafts." Then there are three examples of God stringing-up,
when we might have expected an angel to have done it for Him
– in a later period anyway:

He ... strings his bow and makes it ready.
He has prepared his deadly shafts
and tipped his arrows with fire.

(Psalm 7:12–13)

A hint there of incendiary arrows among the Hebrews? Scholars
are divided, however, as to whether the subject of the sentence
is, in fact, God or the wicked man. A. A. Anderson in the New
Century Bible (1972) favours the latter in view of verse 14. J. W.
Rogerson and J. W. McKay in the Cambridge Bible Commentary
(1977) are undecided. The R.E.B. agrees with Anderson and
makes the fire arrows 'boomerang' against the wicked man: "The

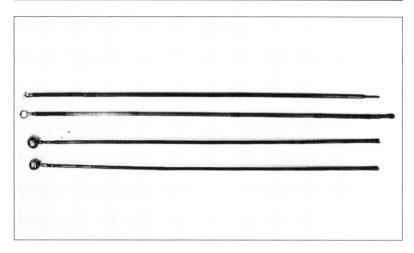

Indian incendiary arrows.
(Courtesy, Simon Archery Collection, The Manchester Museum)

enemy ... strings his bow and makes it ready. It is against himself
he has ..." The other two passages come from Lamentations, the
book which bewails the Fall of Jerusalem in 586 B.C.: "In enmity
he strung his bow" and "he has strung his bow." (Lamentations
2:4 and 3:12) The latter two will be referred to again.

The victims of the Divine shafts in the preceding examples are
not always clear. More obvious targets in the next three instances
are 'evil-doers' and Israel's adversaries. Thus, in connection with
the former: "But God with his arrow shoots them down." (Psalm
64:7) Then, in rather a gory part of the Song of Moses, referring
to enemies: "I will make my arrows drunk with blood." (Deuteronomy 32:42) Again, there is a possible allusion in the 'history' Psalm
78, at verse 48. Strangely enough, the N.E.B. claims a new archery
text, referring to God's treatment of Pharaoh's herds:

> He abandoned their cattle to the plague [or hail]
> and their beasts to the arrows of pestilence [R.E.B. 'to at-
> tacks of'].

The Hebrew *resheph* is normally taken to mean 'thunderbolt', but a god of pestilence, Resheph of the Arrow, was known in ancient Canaan. This is intriguingly paralleled by Apollo's arrows of plague at the beginning of Homer's *Iliad* (1:379–85), dated to the eighth century. All these are instances of the victims we would naturally expect.

God Against Friends

The targets of the Divine arrows, however, can provide some surprises. In half-a-dozen other cases the victims are either Israel herself or 'the good'. Even in the Song of Moses the other reference is anti-Israel:

> I will use up all my arrows on them:
> pangs of hunger, ravages of plague, and bitter pestilence.
>
> (Deuteronomy 32:23–4)

Ezekiel the sixth-century priest-prophet, whose pen is dipped in fire at times (as one scholar put it), uses the same figure of speech: "When I shoot the deadly arrows of famine against you, arrows of destruction, I will shoot to destroy you." (5:16) Returning to the Book of Lamentations, we find a bitter observation in the second lament that the recipients of God's arrows are the Hebrews themselves:

> In enmity he strung his bow;
> he took his stand like an adversary
> and with his strong arm he slew
> all those who had been his delight ...

In the third lament the poet, in a series of troubles too many to have happened to one person, identifies himself with the nation:

> He has strung his bow
> and made me the target for his arrows;

he has pierced my kidneys with shafts
drawn from his quiver.

(Lamentations 2:4 and 3:12–13)

Now to individuals. There are seven Penitential Psalms (No. 51 being the best known perhaps) and it takes a would-be good person to feel the contrition necessary to write one. The author of Psalm 38 considers himself the butt:[28]

For your arrows have rained down on me,
and your hand on me has been heavy.

(verse 2)

This R.E.B. rendering would appear to be closer to the original than the N.E.B. because it avoids the notion of God 'aiming' – see footnote (b) to the latter version. J. Horst, a German scholar, states that in antiquity serious skin diseases were frequently considered to be due to divine or demonic arrows. He mentions the Phoenician deity 'Resheph of the Arrow', referred to above, with whom he compares Apollo in Greek mythology. In the texts from Ugarit (Ras Shamra), on the coast about 180 miles north of Canaan, Resheph is the god of plague.

The other person in the Bible is Job. A datum in the book is that he is a worthy man, but understandably Job complains:

He set me up as his target;
his arrows rained upon me from every side.

(Job 16:12–13)

---

[28] The butt is a "mound of earth or stacked turves against which a shooting mark, or target, is placed. It was widely used from the Middle Ages onward and only gradually disappeared from normal use during the latter half of the nineteenth century with the introduction of the straw target boss." (W. F. Paterson, *Encyclopaedia of Archery* (1984), p. 33–4. The word is derived from the Old French 'but': goal, of unknown origin.)

Nay, worse, Job had earlier protested that God was employing venom:

> The arrows of the Almighty find their mark in me,
> and their poison soaks into my spirit.

(6:4)

Does this reflect a contemporary use of poisoned heads? It may well do so. In any event, to the Greek translator this apparently is libel, perhaps blasphemy, against the Deity, for the Septuagint substitutes *thumos* – anger. Interestingly enough, it adds: "whenever I begin to speak, they pierce me" – as if he feels that God is trying to stifle his arguments. There is a possible reference at 30:11, unique if correct, to *un*stringing a bow to discomfort the owner – again Job is the victim. The New Jerusalem Bible translates:

> And since God has loosened my bow-string and afflicted me,
> they too throw off the bridle in my presence.

and Moffatt in his version renders: "they have unstrung me." The R.V. margin has 'my cord [or bowstring]'; the LXX "for he has opened his quiver and afflicted me"; while N.E.B. and R.E.B. have a version nothing to do with archery. Perhaps the most surprising 'non-reference', which was discovered almost by chance in 'Cruden',[29] is in Job 34:6. Elihu, one of the four so-called comforters, puts into the mouth of Job: "... my wound is incurable, though I am without transgression." The N.E.B. and R.E.B. merely say "my state is desperate". Literally the words are 'my arrow', but seemingly the prefixing of another consonant would give 'my wound' and this was accepted in the A.V., if not

---

[29] *Cruden's Complete Concordance to the Old and New Testaments and the Apocrypha* (London and New York, 3rd Edition, 1769).

before. The LXX has "my arrow is violent" (*biaion to belos mou*), so maybe the Divine shaft did appear in the original Hebrew.

Two Special Texts

This section on God-as-a-Bowman ends with two quite remarkable metaphors. One is from Second Zechariah which that brilliant all-rounder Canon Lowther Clarke described (as was mentioned earlier) as the hardest six chapters in the Old Testament. Professor D. R. Jones, Canon of Durham, dates them after the rebuilding of the Temple in 520–516 but before Nehemiah's arrival in Jerusalem in 444. The text in question depicts the Divine Archer with a bow and arrow – the former being Judah and the arrow being Ephraim: "For I have bent Judah for me, I have filled the bow with Ephraim ... and his arrow shall go forth as the lightning." (Zechariah 9:13–14) This is the R.V. rendering, followed in effect by the R.S.V., Moffatt, and N.J.B. On the other hand, the N.E.B. translates the tribes as vocatives: "For my bow is strung, O Judah; I have laid the arrow to it, O Ephraim." It appears to be half following the Greek Old Testament where Judah seems to be a vocative, but Ephraim certainly is not. The combination of the Joseph tribes (Ephraim and the two divisions of Manasseh on either side of the Jordan) was so powerful that, by synecdoche, the whole northern kingdom of ten tribes was often called Ephraim. Perhaps the clearest example is in Isaiah 7: 2, 8, 9, which relates to the alliance of Syria and Israel against Judah and which was mentioned under 'Isaiah'. It is rather like The Netherlands being known as Holland.

Why does Ephraim appear at all in this period? It was noticed earlier that the concept of 'Ten Lost Tribes' in Assyria is really a misnomer. Certainly Jeremiah (see 3:18; 30:1–3; 31:6 and 9) and Ezekiel (see 37:15–22) only regarded them as 'missing'. The aged

Anna (Luke 2:36) came from the tribe of Asher and the fictional(?) Tobit in the Apocrypha from Naphtali, both in the far north.

The point of the passage is simply that God is to use the united kingdom as a weapon against His enemies – whether Javan ('Greeks' in some versions) signifies the Ionians on the western coast of Asia Minor; the conquests of Alexander the Great; the Seleucids of Syria; the Ptolemies of Egypt; or is merely a generic term for God's enemies among non-Jews.

Second Isaiah (i.e., chapters 40–55) contains four poems called Servant Songs. It is a mystery who the servant is – the nation; the purified part of the nation; an individual? If an individual, Jeremiah? Isaiah of Babylon himself? The second poem has:

> He made my tongue a sharp sword
> and hid me under the shelter of his hand;
> he made me into a polished arrow,
> in his quiver he concealed me.

> (Isaiah 49:2)

Polished? This is the word in R.V., R.S.V., Moffatt, N.E.B. and R.E.B. – the version used here. The N.J.B. has 'sharpened'. An indication as to meaning may be found at Jeremiah 51:11, where R.V. margin gives 'bright', 'clean' as alternatives to 'sharp'. Perhaps a better clue still is to be found in the Septuagint, where the servant described himself as *belos eklekton* – a 'chosen' arrow. At any rate, the significance of the metaphor is twofold: protection and secrecy. In addition, there may well lie the idea of the arrow ranging far – in mission to the Gentile world.

As a postscript to the above, it should be noted that in the famous fourth poem in Isaiah 53 ("the Lord laid upon him the iniquity of us all"), the Church, starting from Philip and the Ethiopian eunuch in Acts 8, has seen a fulfilment of the Suffering Servant – not an exact one, of course – in the life and death of the Saviour. One has only to read the 'Upper Room Discourses' in chapters 13–17 of St John, indeed the Gospel as a whole, to see the close connection of Jesus and His Father. Surely we find this foreshadowed in the close relationship of quiver and arrow – a selected Shaft.

Part II

Thirty figurative references where God is not involved – at least, not as an Archer – have been placed in four categories. The obvious proverbials form the largest group – the tongue being a cruel arrow for example. A kind of sub-division of this is where the wicked or enemies are concerned. Thirdly, there are some semi-metaphorical allusions which have been difficult to classify. In a sense they belong to the literal chapter, but as they have no clear historical context, the question arises where to put them. Finally, there is a group of similar size where faith is involved, and this should prove a happy link with a small section on the New Testament.

Proverbial

In the first category, the contents of which can be put approximately in chronological order, the arrow is the commonest feature in a dozen metaphors and similes, with bow, quiver, and the act of shooting about equal. Probably the oldest simile is that in Hosea, for he wrote in the eighth century, a couple of decades after Amos. He complains that the northerners are turning away from God 'like a deceitful [treacherous] bow.' (Hosea 7:16) Curiously enough, the only other time that this adjective appears with our weapon is also in a criticism of Hebrew loyalty to Yahweh:

> Yet they tested and rebelled against the Most High God,

and did not observe his testimonies,
but turned away and acted treacherously like their fathers;
they twisted like a deceitful bow.

Psalm 78:56–7)

The Greek Old testament has 'twisted' or 'crooked' (*streblos*)
in what is called there the 77th Psalm, which is probably good
enough for the figure of speech desired. However, the Hosea text
has *entetamenon* which means 'stretched'. "They became like a
strung bow" sounds a compliment, whereas the context demands
the reverse. It would have made more sense to say 'unstrung',
but one cannot believe that *enteino* took on the opposite meaning
in the third century B.C. – although there are examples in English
of 'restive', 'let', and maybe 'presently' doing so. In all prob-
ability the translator was accustomed to the word meaning 'bent'
and did not realize the significance for archers.

The Book of Proverbs in its present form is probably third
century, but many of the sayings go back to Hezekiah's time and
to Solomon himself in the tenth century. It so happens that three
of our passages all belong to the second oldest stratum – King
Hezekiah's reign, 716–686 B.C.

Like a club or a sword or a sharp arrow
is a false witness who denounces his friend.

(25:18)

In the second proverb the Hebrew is uncertain, while the Greek
is quite different with a non-archery version. For once, the New
English Bible, with an emendation of the text, is on our side!

Like an archer who shoots at any passer-by
is one who hires a stupid man or a drunkard.

(26:10)

N.J.B. has a similar rendering.
In the same chapter:

A man who deceives another
and then says, "It was only a joke",
is like a madman shooting at random
his deadly darts and arrows.

(Proverbs 26:18–19)

A reference in chapter 7, on the other hand, belongs to the latest stratum – perhaps after 300 B.C. According to Lowther Clarke, this is demanded by the advanced teaching in chapter 8 which speaks of the personification of Wisdom. The content in this section is a series of short essays rather than isolated aphorisms. A vivid picture is painted in one of them by the author who observes from his window a simple and foolish youth on his way to being seduced by a woman while her husband is away.

Unfortunately, some of the Hebrew text containing 'the arrow' in verses 22 and 23 is obscure. In a series of similes it is not certain whether the victim is a bird (so Moffatt), a stag or deer (R.S.V., J.B., and N.I.V.), a madman (N.J.B.) or, in a literal sense, the young adulterer himself! (So N.E.B. and R.E.B.) It is simplest to go by the Greek version: "Ensnared, he followed her – as an ox is led to the slaughter and as a dog to its leads or as a stag struck in the liver by an arrow [*toxeumati*]; and he hastens as a bird into a trap, not knowing that he is running for his life."

The confessor Jeremiah, who ministered from 626 at least to 585, twice credits Yahweh with a metaphor. First, God criticizes Judah's mendacity:

Their tongue is their weapon, a bow ready bent.
Lying, not truth, is master in the land.

(9:3)

The implication in the succeeding lines is that it is sin against Him. In verse 8, however, the trespass is rather against each other, deserving punishment nonetheless:

Their tongue is a cruel arrow,
their mouths speak lies.
One speaks amicably to another,
while inwardly he plans a trap for him.

Psalms 120–134 are in a group called Songs of Ascents, for pilgrims on their way to Zion. In the main they are post-exilic; that is, after 538. One writer in (self-imposed?) banishment, who had been living amid warmongers, bitterly complains about the lies of his enemies. He feels that the slanderous tongue deserves 'a warrior's sharp arrows or red-hot charcoal' (120:4). The New Jerusalem Bible renders: "War arrows made sharp over red-hot charcoal."

The allusion in the other pilgrim song is well known:

Like arrows in the hand of a fighting man
are the sons of a man's youth.
Happy is the man
who has his quiver full of them;
such men shall not be put to shame
when they confront their enemies in court.

(Psalm 127:4–5)

('In the gate' in old versions.) It means that they would be well supported by strong sons in lawsuits and where business was transacted. The New Century Bible comments that when the father gets old, his sons are about to reach their prime. The writer goes on with a challenging observation: Sons "are the first line of God-ordained human defence of the family in times of need ... in more modern terms, one could venture to say that the alternative to a geriatric ward is a God-centred family."

The wisdom of Jesus son of Sirach, better known as 'Ecclesiasticus', was translated from Hebrew to Greek by his grandson in 132 B.C. It is one of the most important books in the Apocrypha and is probably best known for the two passages mentioned later in Appendix II. It yields a couple of texts. The first is characteristic of the sayings in Proverbs:

> As painful as an arrow through the thigh
> is a rumour in the heart of a fool.
>
> (Ecclesiasticus 19:12)

Then in between remarks about a bad wife and a good one ("a silent wife is a gift from the Lord") is advice on keeping watch over a headstrong daughter:

> ... she will open her arms to every embrace,
> and her quiver to the arrow.
>
> (Ecclesiasticus 26:12)

In the Wisdom of Solomon also in the Apocrypha, probably written in the second century, occurs a unique reference. It is at the end of a series of five similes (a shadow, messenger, ship, and bird being the others) on the transitoriness of pride, wealth, and arrogance: "... or as when an arrow is shot at a target, the air is parted and instantly closes up again and no one can tell where it passed through." (Wisdom 5:12)

The last book to be written in the Bible proper is believed to be II Peter – possibly c. A.D. 125 or even later. It may come as a surprise that one work in the Apocrypha, II Esdras (the only book extant in Latin only), is largely coeval. In fact the last two chapters, one of which concerns us, are reckoned to date from as late as c. A.D. 265 and are not believed to be part of the original apocalypse. One reference has already been met, relating to the Almighty, in II Esdras 16:13. Two more are in the same chapter, all three regarding the irresistibility of disasters: "Can any man stop an arrow shot by a strong archer? When the Lord God sends calamities, who can stop them?" "An arrow shot by a powerful archer does not turn back; no more will the calamities be recalled which are let loose against the earth." (II Esdras 16:7–8 and 16)

The Wicked

There follows a sub-section on the use of archery by the wicked, separated from the above because the contents are not proverbial in nature and because they do not have a common theme. All passages are in the Psalms. It will be remembered that there were descriptions of Yahweh stringing-up (Psalm 7 and in Lamentations). In another Psalm, which attempts to deal with the problem of suffering, and which probably dates from the fourth or third century, there is a picture of evil men doing the same.

> The wicked have drawn their swords
> and strung their bows
> to bring low the poor and needy
> and to slaughter honest men.
> Their swords shall pierce their own hearts
> and their bows shall be broken.
>
> (37:14–15)

Again, in another Psalm, there is a portrait of 'baddies' bracing bows and nocking their shafts – the only such allusion in the entire Bible:

> See how the wicked string their bows
> and fit the arrow to the string,
> to shoot down honest men out of the darkness.
>
> (11:2)

Presumably this is simply suggesting the underhand methods of the unjust, as with 64:3–4 below. Dr Lowther Clarke says that there is no internal evidence to fix the date. Very tentatively may one speculate that it is by the author of Psalm 37 above and hence of the same period? Not only is the archery language similar, but also the theme of innocent suffering.

Another poet complains:

> For I lie down among lions, man-eaters,
> whose teeth are spears and arrows
> and whose tongues are sharp swords.
>
> (57:4)

Contrary to what one has come to expect, the N.E.B. has brought in an interesting reference in Psalm 55 – the one that contains "Oh for the wings of a dove!" – which has a parallel in a Greek play. The writer, having complained bitterly about wickedness in the city and the taunts of a close friend, declares:

> But I will call upon God;
> the Lord will save me.
> Evening and morning and at noon
> I nurse my woes, and groan.
> He has heard my cry, he rescued me
> and gave me back my peace,
> when they beset me like archers,
> massing against me,
> like Ishmael and the desert tribes
> and those who dwell in the East ...
>
> (verses 18 and 19)

A footnote states that 'when ... archers' is the probable reading and that the Hebrew is obscure – the usual formula. Rogerson and McKay in their three-volume paperback commentary on the Psalms for the New English Bible version claim that the translators have used some ingenious conjectures to obtain the allusions to 'archers' and 'the desert tribes of the East'. The Ishmaelites in north-west Arabia were believed to have descended from Abraham via his Egyptian slave-wife Hagar. According to one tradition which the writer heard in the Holy Land, she was a captured widowed queen, possibly acquired from Pharaoh (Genesis 12:16). It will be remembered that Ishmael himself became an archer and he too married an Egyptian (21:20–21). In *Antigone* (*c.* 441 B.C.), Sophocles put similar words into the mouth of Creon, King of Thebes in succession to Oedipus. He has had Antigone, the late monarch's daughter and his own intended daughter-in-law, walled up alive for burying her brother against strict orders. Teiresias, the blind prophet, and others vehemently urge Creon to release her. He retorts: "Old man, you are all shooting at me like archers at a target." (*toxotai skopou toxeuete* – lines 1033–4)

It has to be said, however, that the recent revisers rejected the 'probable reading', abolishing both archers and Ishmael.

Psalm 64 has two features to notice:

> Hide me from the factions of the wicked,
> from the turbulent mob of evildoers,
> who sharpen their tongues like swords
> and wing their cruel words like arrows,
> to shoot down the innocent from cover,
> shooting suddenly, themselves unseen.

(verses 2–4)

A. A. Anderson, mentioned earlier, having first said that the writer may have been thinking of slanders and false accusations, makes the fascinating suggestion that it could relate to magic spells or curses. He goes on to say that the 'shooting suddenly' implies that the enemies strike unexpectedly, resorting to sorcery perhaps – hence the secretiveness of their activities. As was seen earlier in verse 7, "God with his arrow shoots them down, and sudden is their overthrow." In other words, the judgement of the Almighty repays in kind. As the Cambridge Commentators put it, sin has a boomerang effect and rebounds on the head of its perpetrators.

The other thing worth commenting on is the jibe about shooting from cover, unseen (LXX 'unafraid'). There are echoes of this in two fifth-century Greek plays. In Sophocles' *Ajax* (440s B.C.), Menelaus sneers at Teucer – and it is good to hear the master-bowman answering the King back (lines 1120 ff.). In Euripides' *The Madness of Hercules* (c. 416 B.C.), there is a dialogue on the ethics of archery. Lycus attacks the cowardly bow and exalts the spear – criticising the exploits of Hercules. This is followed by a lengthy defence of archery by Amphitryon (lines 159–64; 188–205).

Miscellany

There are four miscellaneous passages which defy analysis. They are semi-literal, yet they cannot be placed in a sure historical setting. Two are in 'royal' psalms, one relates somehow to northern marksmanship (or rather, lack of it), while the fourth is about penetration and the crocodile.

After a thanksgiving for blessings to the king, Psalm 21 contains a prediction of future triumph over his enemies:

> ... but you will catch them round the shoulders (?)
> and will aim with your bowstrings at their faces.
>
> (verse 12)

The employment of string, instead of bow or arrow, is unique.

In place of the queried line, R.E.B. has 'and force them to turn in flight', which it puts second. Since there is now no footnote, it may be that the meaning of the words has been discovered.

Psalm 45 is specifically addressed to a warrior king, but in exaggeratedly flattering terms. It is possible, perhaps probable, that the monarch eulogized is King Ahab (874–853 B.C.) for his consort is alluded to as 'daughter of Tyre' and 'a king's daughter' both of which Jezebel was. Maybe it was a wedding ode early in his reign, for it could hardly have been composed after the judicial murder of Naboth whose vineyard Ahab had coveted. For once, perhaps, the context is more interesting than the text:

> Your right hand shall show you a scene of terror:
> your sharp arrows flying, nations beneath your feet,
> the courage of the king's foes melting away!
>
> (verses 4–5)

Rogerson and McKay in the Cambridge Bible Commentary maintain that the N.E.B. emendation is too radical and they suggest a simpler re-arrangement: "Your arrows are sharp; they fall into the heart of the king's foes. Nations are subject to you." For the last line of verse 4, N.J.B. as a conjecture has: "Stretch the bowstring tight, lending terror to your right hand."

The commentators are puzzled over:

> The men of Ephraim, bowmen all and marksmen,
> turned and ran in the hour of battle.
>
> (Psalm 78:9)

It appears at first glance that it relates to the cowardice of a particular tribe in a fight of which we have no record. However, 'Ephraim' surely means here the northern kingdom of Israel, as we saw earlier, especially as it is contrasted with Judah in verses 67–8. A harder question is whether it is literal or figurative. The present writer believes that there may be a clue in the lines before and after verse 9. The context is severe criticism, presumably by a southerner, of Israel's disobedience and rebellion against Yahweh. The next lines read: "They had not kept God's covenant and had refused to live by his law." Is not this giving the reason for Israel's turning and running? For 'battle' read 'war' – the final conflict with Assyria in 721? Is not the Psalmist implying that if the northern kingdom had kept God's commandments, they would have shot the heathen to pieces as the Parthians did to the Roman invaders at the Battle of Carrhae in 53 B.C?

Provided that the N.E.B. translation of 'clan' in verse 67 is correct (and not a word which implies 'shrine'), Rogerson and McKay come to the same conclusion – see p. 151 and also p. 143

of the Cambridge Commentary. A. A. Anderson has a long entry on the problem in the New Century Bible (p. 562), discussing the purpose and date of the second longest Psalm. Was it for services or as propaganda? Was it to justify the leadership of Judah over Ephraim, of worship at Jerusalem over the shrine at Shiloh? Some scholars date it before the Division of the Kingdom *c.* 930 (as there is no reference to it), while Anderson himself prefers a time nearer 600 for half-a-dozen reasons. With the latter view the present writer concurs, of course, and so, it would appear, do the Cambridge commentators. Could it, perhaps, be later still? The expression 'kissers of the bow' occurs here, and elsewhere only in I and II Chronicles – which are dated *c.* 300 B.C.

Lastly, there is a long passage in the Book of Job about an animal, when it is stated that "the arrow – *lit.* 'son of the bow' – cannot make him flee." (41:28) There is general agreement that Leviathan, the creature in question, is the crocodile. Oddly enough, the New English Bible also relates the arrow text to the same animal, but by a different route.[30] It is tempting to infer something about arrow penetration in the fourth century B.C. It would be in vain. The author is concerned to show that the crocodile can resist anything, except its Maker.

---

[30] The New English Bible transposes Job 41:1–6, when Leviathan is mentioned, to the end of chapter 39 but it translates it as 'whale'. The same conclusion for our purposes is reached, however, because it renders Behemoth in Job 40:15 by 'crocodile'. The translators appear to have accepted Professor Sir Godfrey Driver's view of the two words, published in 1956. Behemoth is otherwise believed to be the hippopotamus (cognate with the Egyptian word for water-ox?) or possibly the elephant.

Faith

In the last section are five passages which are concerned to a greater or lesser extent with faith in Yahweh. Most of the references in 'Job' are negative (twice he is a target) and it is good to find our hero making a positive statement:

> Then I thought "I shall die in my nest,
> and I shall multiply my days as the sand,
> my roots spread out to the waters,
> with the dew all night on my branches,
> my glory fresh with me,
> and my bow ever new in my hand."
>
> (29:18–20)

Job is wistfully stating his hopes for the future, including the maintenance of his physical powers. Compare Genesis 49:24 – "his bow abode in strength", if indeed this is the correct reading. Oddly enough, the New English Bible brings in 'arrow' and without stating the basis for the conjecture:

> with the bow always new in my grasp
> and the arrow ever ready to my hand.

Moffatt (who has no mention of a bow as it happens), N.J.B. and N.E.B. consider that some sentences about Job's prestige have been misplaced and have put verses 21 to 25 to follow verse 10. This has the effect of making the archery text in verse 20 the climax to chapter 29, rather than the comparison of a king among his troops.

Returning to the Psalms, three more positive allusions can be found. The first asserts:

> I will not trust in my bow,
> nor will my sword win me the victory.
>
> (44:6)

It is suggested that this verse, at least, was spoken on behalf of the congregation by a religious or military leader. Various ideas have been put forward as to dating. The present writer considers that Sennacherib's invasion of the south in 701 is the likely occasion, verse 11 referring to the deportation of the northern kingdom two decades before.

The 91st was once called the 'A.R.P. (Air Raid Precautions) Psalm in World War II, because of its theme of Divine protection. The sentence reads:

> You will not fear the terror of the night,
> nor the arrow that flies by day.

(verse 5)

According to Canon Lowther Clarke, the night-monster in this Psalm is probably the Lilith of Isaiah 34:14, while the arrow was a demon active by day, sunstroke perhaps, a similar conception to Apollo's arrow.

The last Psalm is a sad little poem, including the archery text – for the standard is to be raised not for attack but for retreat:

> Thou has set up a banner for those who fear thee,
> to rally to it from the bow.

(60:4)

There is doubt about the text. The quotation from the R.S.V. is based on the Greek, Syriac, and St Jerome – followed by Moffatt, N.J.B. and now the R.E.B. The R.V. margin has "That they may flee from before the bow", while R.V. main text and N.E.B. have no archery motif. The Cambridge Bible points out that *koset* occurs only here in the Old Testament. It may be an Aramaic form of the Hebrew word for bow. The final consonant is slightly different.

To end with, there is a reference in Hannah's Prayer (which

bears a superficial resemblance to St Mary's Magnificat) which she was said to have uttered after the birth of Samuel in the eleventh century.

> The bow of the mighty has become feeble
> and the feeble have girded themselves with strength.
>
> (I Samuel 2:4)

The Greek version is given here because the same word for weak or feeble is used in both parts, which brings out the contrast nicely. Yet again the New English Bible rejects an archery passage, claiming that the Hebrew is obscure.

Some Notes on the Hebrew

THE usual word for arrow is ḥēṣ, from the root ḥṣṣ 'divide'. There is a rare parallel form ḥēṣî derived from the root ḥṣh which is found in the second part of the Jonathan and David episode (I Samuel 20:36–8) and in the assassination of King Joram, "and the arrow went out at his heart." (II Kings 9:24) Verbs for shooting arrows include rbb "The archers shot at him", i.e., the tribe of Joseph (Genesis 49:23); "And he [God] sent out his arrows and scattered them." (Psalm 18:14) This gives rise to the term rab an archer; rbh relating to Abraham's son Ishmael (Genesis 21:20); yrh comes in the Jonathan and David event (I Samuel 20:36–7) and the King of Assyria shall not 'shoot an arrow there'. (II Kings 19:32) There are participial forms yôrîm, môrîm signifying archers, and šlḥ send (I Samuel 20:20, if the text is genuine).

The word for bow is qešeṭ. The regular word for bending is 'tread' – drk. (By a curious transference, arrows are said to be 'trodden' in Psalm 64:3 translated as "And have aimed their arrows, even bitter words.") The word mšk, draw, is also employed.

The term yeter, cord, which is used for a bowstring – the wicked nock their arrow on the string (Psalm 11:2) and God loosing Job's bowstring (Job 30:11) – could also be a cord for binding a man as in the case of Samson (Judges 16:7–9) or possibly a tent-cord as in Job 4:21; mētār "Thou shalt make ready with thy bowstrings against the face of them" (Psalm 21:12) can also mean a tent-cord as in Jeremiah 10:20, as well as a bowstring.

Arrows were kept in a quiver, ašhpâ – a quiverful of children (Psalm 127:5), the Suffering Servant in God's quiver (Isaiah 49:2), while 'sons of the quiver' mean arrows (Lamentations 3:13). They might be shot at a 'mark' or target, *mattārâ*, God setting Job up, he felt, as His target (Job 16:12); so thought the writer of Lamentations 3:12; it also occurs in I Samuel 20:20 above.

Epilogue

U NDERSTANDABLY, the references to Archery in the New Testament are few – so scarce, in fact, that this section is not called a chapter.

The only certain passage is in the 'Apocalypse', probably written in the A.D. 90s. Here there is a rare mention in the Bible of a horsed archer: "And I saw, and behold, a white horse and he who sat on it had a bow; and a crown was given to him, and he went out conquering and to conquer." (Revelation 6:2) It is believed that this alludes to the Parthians who had defeated the Romans ('conquering') in A.D. 62 and were likely to have future victories ('and to conquer'). If the link with these mounted bowmen is correct, it might suggest that this section belongs to an early stratum of the Book of Revelation. It would date to the time of Nero in the sixties when the Parthian success was fresher in the mind. That it is this emperor is proved almost beyond doubt by giving values to the Hebrew letters in Neron Caesar which produces 666, 'the number of the Beast' in Revelation 13:18. It also works with a variant reading 616, if one spells it Nero Caesar as we do.

Almost certain is 'arrow' in St. Paul's charge from prison c. A.D. 60 to his converts in Ephesus and other cities of Asia Minor. In the middle of the sixfold panoply for spiritual warfare, he writes: "… taking the shield of faith, with which you can extinguish all the flaming missiles of the evil one." (Ephesians 6:16) With perhaps over-caution, *belos* (which only occurs here) has been rendered by the generic word 'missile', which was employed for such extremes as a mountain peak hurled by a giant and a thrown chamber-pot. More orthodox Greek words for

"Vision of a White Horse", painted by Philip James de Loutherbourg (1740–1812) in 1798. Based on Revelation 6:2, the mounted bowman may reflect the Parthian invasion of A.D. 62. Note the rider with two-handed sword on a red steed who is mentioned in the next verse.

The artist has depicted splendidly a Tatar bow, including siyah and bridge for the string near the nocks. However, from the archer's viewpoint, several other features are incorrect: the draw is not central on the string and the anchor-point is somewhat too low on the body; a poor attempt has been made on an oriental thumb-lock, when the arrow should have been on the other side of the bow; the arrowhead is too large. Although both riders give the impression of tremendous power, the head of the horsed archer would be more appropriate for the Queen of the Amazons. (Courtesy, The Tate Gallery) arrow were *oïstos*, *ios*, and *toxeuma*, but *belos* was frequently used. Indeed, it has been noticed here with this significance in the Greek Old Testament. Moreover, the 'fiery' adjective does suggest a longer range weapon than javelin or dart, which might uncomfortably involve the thrower. There appears no reason to doubt the 'flaming' or 'burning' arrows of the New English Bible and the New Jerusalem Bible respectively. The only other mention of a fiery shaft in Scripture was a metaphor in Psalm 7:13.

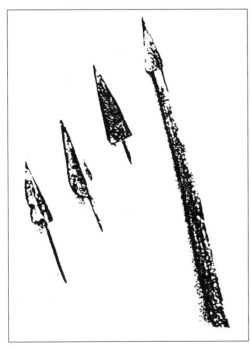

Four of the numerous iron arrowheads which were found near a Zealot warrior at Masada, near the west coast of the Dead Sea. One head still has its original wooden or reed shaft.

The 'palace fortress', built by Herod the Great, eventually fell to the Romans in A.D. 73 after the Jews had withstood siege for an heroic eight months. [Illustration from Yigael Yadin's *Masada* (London, 1966), p. 57] (Courtesy, the Estate of Yigael Yadin.)

It is worth digressing here to point out that incendiary arrows were used in Abyssinia, now called by its old name Ethiopia, in the Second World War against the Italians. The bow had at least two other uses and it is curious that this ancient weapon, which goes back to Palaeolithic times, was employed in the same war as the atomic bomb.

To return to the early Christian Church. The 'Gospel of Thomas' was discovered in 1945–6 in Upper Egypt. It contains 114 alleged Sayings of

Christ in Coptic, dated *c.* A.D. 400, although the Greek original is believed to be as early as *c.* A.D. 150. The first half of No. 48, in the Leipoldt enumeration, runs as follows: "Jesus said: 'It is impossible for a man to mount two horses and stretch two bows, and it is impossible for a slave to serve two masters. Either he will honour the one and despise the other (or he will hate the one and love the other)'." Is it a genuine Saying? There are two points which suggest that such a remark was not impossible. In the first place, the reference to horses and bows is connected to the canonical Saying in Luke 16:13 (= Matthew 6:24) in the hypothetical document known as 'Q'.[31] Secondly, the allusion has a proverbial ring about it and is clearly innocent of the Gnostic tendency of the collection.

The last two items refer to missing the target – and to reaching it. The Greek verb *hamartano* 'to sin' also means 'to miss the mark'. Which sense came first is not absolutely certain. The present writer agrees with Mr. T. G. Rosenmeyer of Iowa State University that the 'aiming' one is secondary. Working from examples in Homer in the eighth century B.C., the root meaning appears to be something like 'to be deficient'. If so, then one might hazard the guess that it means to miss the mark by falling short – i.e., by being deficient in power. (This conception of falling short of one's ideals is complemented by 'transgressing', which means overstepping the mark.) In the New Testament *hamartano* is applied to sinning against God (the Woman caught in Adultery, John 8:11) or man (Matthew 18:15) or against both God and man at the same time (The Prodigal Son, Luke 15:18).

---

[31] Q is an assumed document, consisting mainly of Sayings of Jesus (only some three narratives) which Luke and Matthew have used, but which are not in Mark. 'Q' (believed to be from the German *quelle*: source) was coined by Weiss in 1881, but was elaborated by Professor Adolf Harnack and Sir John Hawkins about the first decade of this century.

It can also refer to offending the civil power (Paul before the Governor, Acts 25:8; and I Peter 2:20), without the idea of 'sin'.

Finally, there is a possible reference – and a splendid one with which to end – in St Paul's letter to his especial friends, the Philippians. It was written a year or so after Ephesians when he was still in prison. While it must be admitted that the 'goal' of several modern versions sounds today more suitable, *skopos* can in fact mean 'target'. Indeed, the Authorized or King James Version of 1611 has the synonym 'mark'.

... forgetting what lies behind and stretching forward to what lies ahead, I press on towards the target for the prize of the upward call of God in Christ Jesus.

Philippians 3:13–14

Archery References

In order to be comprehensive, all passages are given, even where the text is suspect. Where practicable, there is a brief mention of content.

The Old Testament

Genesis	9:13–16	rainbow (cf. Ezekiel 1:28)
	21:16 and 20	Ishmael
	27:3	Esau's hunting
	48:22	Jacob to Joseph
	49:23–4	Archers v. Joseph
Exodus	19:13	execution
Numbers	24:8	Balaam's prophecy
Deuteronomy	32:23 and 42	God's arrows
Joshua	24:12	'hornet', not bow
Judges	5:11	Song of Deborah
	16:7–9	Samson's bowstrings
I Samuel	2:4	Hannah's Song
	18:4	Jonathan's gift
	20:20–40	his secret sign
	31:3	Saul wounded
II Samuel	1:18 and 22	David's Lament
	8:7	golden quivers?
	11:20 and 24	Uriah the Hittite
	22:15	God's arrows
	22:35	bronze bow
I Kings	22:34	Ahab's death
II Kings	6:22	Elisha and Syrians

	9:24 and 27	assassination of Joram by Jehu; Ahaziah shot also
	13:15–19	arrow through window; arrows striking floor
	19:32	Sennacherib
I Chronicles	5:18	Trans-Jordan tribes
	8:40	150 Benjaminites
	10:3	(= I Samuel 31:3)
	12:2	David's archers
II Chronicles	14:8	King Asa's bowmen
	17:17	King Jehoshaphat's bowmen
	18:33	(= I Kings 22:34)
	26:14	King Uzziah's bows
	26:15	ditto arrow ballistas?
	35:23	Josiah's death
Nehemiah	4:13 and 16	defence of Jerusalem
Job	6:4	poisoned arrows – figurative
	16:12 and 13	Job as target
	20:24 and 25	bronze bow
	29:20	'bow renewed'
	30:11	bow 'unstrung'
	34:6	arrow 'incurable'
	39:23	quiver on horse
	41:28	arrow v. crocodile
Psalm	7:12 and 13	fire arrows – figurative
	11:2	nocking
	18:14 and 34	(= II Samuel 22:15 and 35)
	21:12	bowstrings
	37:14 and 15	
	38:2	
	44:6	
	45:5	
	46:9	
	55:18–19	

	57:4	
	58:7	
	60:4	
	64:3, 4 and 7	
	76:3	
	77:17	
	78:9	Ephraim
	78:48	
	78:57	
	91:5	
	120:4	
	127:4 and 5	quiverful of children
	144:6	
Proverbs	7:23	
	25:18	
	26:10 and 18–19	
Isaiah	5:28	
	7:24	
	13:18	
	21:15 and 17	
	22:3 and 6	
	37:33	(= II Kings 19:32)
	41:2	Cyrus the Persian
	49:2	Suffering Servant
	66:19	
Jeremiah	4:29	
	5:16	
	6:23	
	9:3 and 8	
	46:9	
	49:35	
	50:9, 14, 29, 42	
	51:3, 11, 56	
Lamentations	2:4	

	3:12 and 13	
Ezekiel	5:16	
	21:21–2	divination
	39:3 and 9	Gog and Magog; firewood
Hosea	1:5 and 7	
	2:18	
	7:16	
Amos	2:15	
Habakkuk	3:9	bare bow
	3:11	
Zechariah	9:10	battle-bow
	9:13–14	Judah and Ephraim
	10:4	battle-bow

The Apocrypha

II Esdras	16:7, 13, 16	
Judith	2:15	horsed archers
	9:7	bow in prayer
Wisdom	5:12 and 21	
Ecclesiasticus	19:12	
	26:12	
I Maccabees	9:11	death of Judas
II Maccabees	10:30	five heavenly archers

The New Testament

Revelation	6:2	mounted bowman
Ephesians	6:16	incendiary arrows
(Gospel of Thomas 48)		(drawing two bows)
Luke	15:18	missing the mark
Philippians	3:14	the Target

Appendix I

The Revolution

c. 930 B.C.

THE more-or-less united kingdom of Saul, David and Solomon split up on the latter's death. To appreciate the two monarchies of Judah and Israel, it might be helpful to explain the cause of the division.

The wisdom of Solomon has become proverbial. He chose it in the dream he had at Gibeon (six miles north-west of Jerusalem) and, for not asking for 'long life or riches or the life of your enemies', God in fact gave him wealth and honour as well. On the debit side, however, there was the self-indulgence with 700 wives (so-called 'princesses' – but where were so many royal families to provide them?) and 300 concubines; the later lapse into foreign religious cults; and forced labour.

In charge of the latter operations in central Palestine was an able and industrious young man called Jeroboam son of Nebat ('who made Israel to sin'), whom Solomon himself had promoted. Once on leaving Jerusalem he was joined by Ahijah of Shiloh, a prophet, who was wearing a new robe. When they were alone, Ahijah tore this garment into twelve pieces. In an act of what is known as 'prophetic symbolism', he told Jeroboam to take ten, adding in God's name: "I am about to tear the kingdom from the hand of Solomon, and will give you ten tribes." Either they were not alone or one of them talked, for Solomon got to hear of it and Jeroboam had to flee for his life to Pharaoh Shishak.

It took two decades to build the Temple and the Palace. By the time Solomon died, the people had had enough so they summoned Jeroboam back from Egypt. He led a delegation to Rehoboam, Solomon's son, who was at Shechem (present-day Nablus) expecting to be made king. Jeroboam requested that the work load be reduced – and for three days the nation must have held its breath. King Rehoboam consulted Solomon's 'privy council' of old men who advised him that he should serve the people and speak fair words – and they would be his servants for ever. Rehoboam then asked his contemporaries for their opinion. The response must rank as one of the worst pieces of advice ever given to a sovereign. They recommended that the forced labour actually should be increased, with the infamous footnote, "My father chastised you with whips, but I will chastise you with scorpions" – presumably meaning some form of cat-o'-nine-tails. The reaction was instant: "What portion have we in David? We have no inheritance in the son of Jesse. To your tents, O Israel! Look now to your own house, David."

When Adoram the chief taskmaster was stoned to death, Rehoboam took to his chariot and escaped to Jerusalem – about thirty miles to the south. He was instructed via a prophet not to attempt to get Israel back, so he had to settle for Judah and Benjamin only. Meanwhile Jeroboam made Shechem his capital and set up shrines – alas, with golden calves to worship 'which made Israel to sin' – at Dan in the north and at Bethel (only ten miles north of Jerusalem). This was to discourage his people from going back to Jerusalem for festivals and so running the risk of returning to the House of David.

Appendix II

The Apocrypha

SOME PARTS of the Apocrypha were accepted as canonical by the early Church and cited by many early Chistian writers. However, the New Testament itself, which shows a knowledge of it, never quotes any of it as Scripture. Attitudes vary enormously: (a) The Jewish authorities themselves are believed to have destroyed the Hebrew originals some time after the Fall of Jerusalem in A.D. 70, evidently regarding it as second-class Scripture. (b) The Roman Catholic Church at the Council of Trent, A.D. 1545–63, made no distinction in rank with the rest of the Bible, though it placed three books as a supplement after the New Testament. (c) The Greek Church at the Council of Jerusalem in A.D. 1672 accepted Wisdom, Ecclesiasticus, Tobit, and Judith as canonical, reversing its previous view. (d) The British and Foreign Bible Society, which had a largely Protestant background, refused in A.D. 1827 to circulate it. (e) The Anglican Church, as might be expected, takes very much a midway position. Article VI of 'The Thirty-Nine', A.D. 1563, approves of it 'for example of life and instruction of manners', but not for establishing any doctrine. The Lectionaries of A.D. 1549, 1871, and 1922 all have First Lessons from the Apocrypha, while the Bible presented to the Sovereign at Coronation contains the collection.

The Apocrypha consists of fifteen books – fourteen in the Authorized and Revised Versions, because Baruch and Jeremiah are combined:

I Esdras	He is the Ezra of the Old Testament. The chief interest to non-specialists is the story of the three pages to King Darius.
II Esdras	The only book in the 'extended' Bible which survives in Latin only. It is an 'Apocalypse', such as Daniel in the Old Testament and Revelation in the New, of the Christian era, by various writers from A.D. 70 to perhaps as late as A.D. 250.
Tobit	An enchanting novel, involving Archangel Raphael, which contains a most unusual romance. James Bridie based his play *Tobias and the Angel* on it. Two pieces of external evidence date it to the Persian period (530s–330s B.C.), much earlier than previously thought.
Judith	A devout, beautiful and rich Jewish widow delivers her people by assassinating the enemy generalissimo. Almost certainly it dates from the Maccabaean period in the second century B.C.

The Rest of the Book of Esther

'Esther' in the Bible proper makes no reference to God, prayer, or worship. The Jews in Alexandria sought to remedy this by producing a revised edition, in or before 114 B.C., which does contain religious teaching.

The Wisdom of Solomon

Chapters 1–9, influenced by Greek philosophy, are a magnificent portrayal of the demands and rewards of Wisdom, its nature and powers. Chapters 10–19, although regarded as relatively inferior, nevertheless contain scores of gems.

Ascription to Solomon is a literary device. It was written in Alexandria any time between the second century B.C. and A.D. 40, for it was used by St. Paul and perhaps by other N.T. authors. (They never quote it *directly*, as was said at the beginning.) The book contains the funeral lesson "The souls of the righteous are in the hand of God".

Ecclesiasticus or The Wisdom of Jesus (Joshua) son of Sirach (51 chapters)

was written in Hebrew and translated into Greek by his grandson in 132 B.C. It is an anthology similar to the Book of Proverbs, but more attractive as the sayings are often expanded. 'Let us now praise famous men ...' and 'Honour the physician ...' come from it.

Baruch   The setting is in troubled years after a national disaster. Most of the book expresses deep religious fervour in which, in a spirit of faith and resignation, enemies are to be prayed for. Baruch was Jeremiah's secretary, but the date cannot be earlier than second century B.C. and was probably published in its present form after the Fall of Jerusalem in A.D. 70.

The Epistle of Jeremiah

This purports to be a letter written by the prophet Jeremiah to the Jews about to be deported to Babylon in 586 B.C. It is a warning against the worship of Tammuz and idolatry in general. It is yet another literary device, for the book appears to date itself to the fourth century.

The Song of the Three Holy Children

> Possibly to be dated 100 B.C., it was inserted in
> the Greek version of Daniel 3 in the Bible proper
> after verse 23. It is ascribed to Shadrach, Meshach
> and Abednego in Nebuchadnezzar's 'burning
> fiery furnace'. (It is sung in Anglican churches at
> Matins – the Benedicite – as an alternative and
> can be said by a Roman Catholic priest to himself
> after Mass.)

The History of Susanna

> Two evil judges get her condemned to death on
> a false charge of adultery. Daniel saves her by
> cross-examining them separately – which is the
> origin of 'A Daniel come to judgement' in Shake-
> speare's *The Merchant of Venice*. The story,
> often represented in sacred art, is almost certainly
> early first century B.C.

Bel and the Dragon (Snake)

> This is a third addition to the Book of Daniel, of
> unknown date, about two idols. It involves a sim-
> ple detective story (footprints), an explosion, and
> a vertical take-off.

The Prayer of Manasseh

> According to II Chronicles 33, this seventh-cen-
> tury King of Judah was imprisoned in Babylon
> by the Assyrians for a time. Reference is made to
> his repentance (verses 12 and 13) and to his
> prayer (verse 18). Though a 'little classic of peni-
> tential devotion', it is not thought to be genuine

– it is first found in a Christian document of the third century A.D.

I Maccabees   A military history whose climax is the revolt against the Syrian overlord Antiochus IV Epiphanes in 168 B.C., the achievement of independence, and the re-dedication of the Temple three years later.

II Maccabees   It is rhetorical in style, exaggerated and full of portents. It is useful for the study of Jewish religion just before the Christian era, especially in its teaching about martyrdom and resurrection. Its relation to I Maccabees is possibly to be compared with that of Chronicles to Kings.

I am grateful to Professor J. C. Dancy for reading through my pages on the Apocrypha and for making a valuable suggestion and half-a-dozen comments. Before becoming Professor of Education at the University of Exeter, Mr Dancy was Headmaster in turn of Lancing College, Sussex, and of Marlborough College, Wiltshire.

Bibliography

General

Peake's Commentary on the Bible (2nd Edition, 1962)
W. K. Lowther Clarke, *Concise Bible Commentary* (1952)

Also consulted:

A New Commentary on Holy Scripture (1928), Edited by Gore, Goudge, and Guillaume
The One Volume Bible Commentary (1909), Edited by J. R. Dummelow.
Occasional use has also been made of *The Cambridge Bible for Schools and Colleges* and of *The Century Bible* on individual books of the Scriptures.

Abbreviations of Versions

LXX — The Old Testament in Greek (see the first footnote)
A.V. — The Authorized (or King James') Version (1611)
R.V. — The Revised Version (1885)
Moffatt — translation by James Moffatt (1935)
R.S.V. — The Revised Standard Version (Old Testament 1952)
J.B. — The Jerusalem Bible (1966)
N.E.B. — The New English Bible (Old Testament 1970)
N.I.V. — The New International Version (1979)
N.J.B. — The New Jerusalem Bible (2nd Ed., 1985)
R.E.B. — The Revised English Bible (1989)

Acknowledgements

The Scripture quotations contained herein from the Revised Standard Version of the Bible, copyright 1946, 1952, 1971 by the Division of Christian Education of the National Council of the Churches of Christ in the U.S.A. are used by permission.

The Jerusalem Bible published and © 1966, 1967 and 1968 by Darton Longman & Todd Ltd., and Doubleday & Co. Inc. is used by permission of the publishers.

The New Jerusalem Bible published and © 1985 by Darton Longman & Todd Ltd., and Doubleday & Co. Inc. is used by permission of the publishers.

Quotations from The New English Bible © 1970 by permission of Oxford and Cambridge University Presses.

Quotations from The Revised English Bible © 1989 by permission of Oxford and Cambridge University Presses.

The tribal map © The British and Foreign Bible Society 1967.

The maps of the Holy Land and of the Persian Empire are reproduced from the Oxford Bible Atlas, Third Edition, with the permission of the publishers, Oxford University Press.

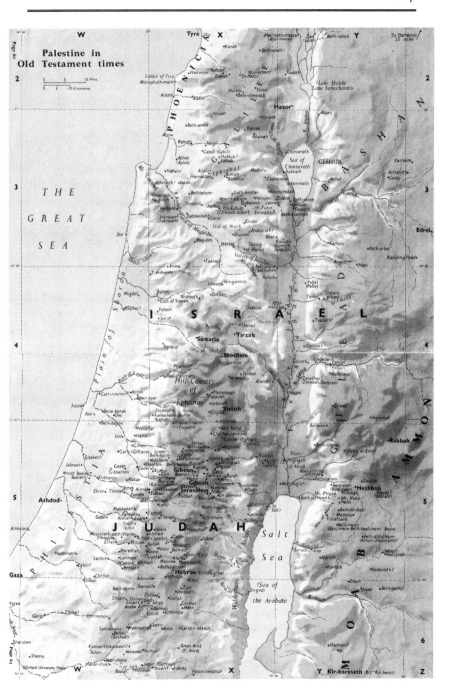

Palestine in
Old Testament times

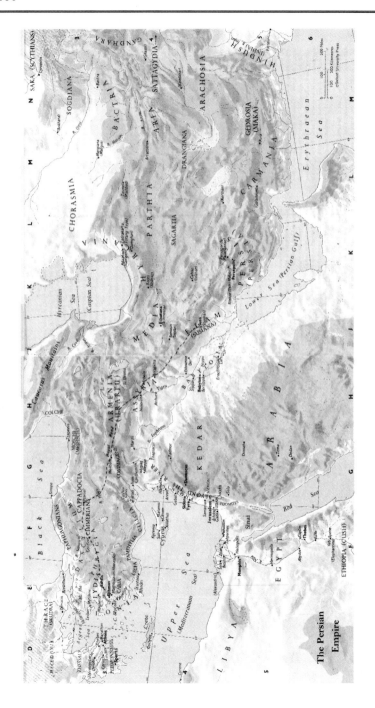

The Persian Empire